知识就是力量

Knowledge is Power

Table of Contents

Introduction:

This book was written to assist any player in performing better on the racquetball court. Whether you are a recreational player or an aspiring Pro Tour hopeful, "**Percentage Racquetball**" will greatly improve your ability to beat other players. This system is built around playing the percentages, which work out in your favor the majority of the time. This makes your job on the court much easier. This system will show you how to win even if you are not playing at your peak. The philosophies contained within are applicable for all levels of play.

The information contained in the book is a compilation of 20+ years of trial and error, success and failure. My goal is to help you avoid some of the mistakes that I made, and expedite your journey to your highest level of play. The information contained in this book will make your job on the court <u>easier</u>. **The system revealed in this book never fails.** You may fail within the system by skipping the ball or making a bad decision, but **the system never fails.** The correct strokes, footwork, court position and shot selection set forth in this book will help you become more consistent and win more matches. Reading this book and adopting the principles within will make you a better player, regardless of your current ability level.

As a coach, I have come to the conclusion that in terms of mechanics, I teach people to do LESS, not more. Most people add extra things into their swing, and this means that have more areas in which to make a mistake. *My approach is MINIMALISM…the less you have to get right the easier it is to be right!* I am sure this book will add to your knowledge base of things you bring to a game, but in terms of mechanics, we will be learning to do less, not more.

Thoughts:

If you choose to pursue racquetball as an athlete, you must appreciate that being an athlete is not a part-time thing. It is like Vince Lombardi said, "Winning isn't a sometimes thing, it is an everyday thing." You must learn to see each day as an opportunity to improve... as an athlete and as a person. In my opinion, athletics is really about mastery of the **self**, and not mastery of a certain skill. The skill(s) that are mastered are a by-product of the journey. Personal discipline is one of the critical skills to be developed. To live and train like a champion, to be a person of integrity and honor, to follow your dreams and *realize* your goals is one of life's greatest accomplishments and one of the most satisfying experiences. The best thing I ever did to improve my racquetball game was to tighten up my life and rid myself of all the draining things and people that would be a distraction from my journey. It was difficult, but worth every bit of effort, and then some. I am the man I am today because of this journey.

A progressive spirit is always opposed by people who are too afraid to try or who have tried a little and failed. The world is riddled with nay-sayers. Those people will do their best to keep you where you are, thereby keeping themselves in their comfort zone. If you begin to improve and leave them behind, that is yet another reminder to them of their inability to do the same. I am not saying you must become a champion at racquetball to live this way. Instead, live this way and you will be a champion, regardless of your accomplishments on the court. If someone doubts you, don't believe them. ***Believe in yourself.***

To quote Lombardi, "The quality of a person's life is in direct proportion to their commitment to excellence, regardless of their field or chosen endeavor." When excellence is your goal, wins and losses are less important than the big picture view of living the journey.

Part of my commitment to excellence was to reach the Professional ranks. I joined the IRT Tour in 1994, and achieved a career high ranking of 18 by 1997. I can honestly state that I have achieved my racquetball goals.

There was no, "But I don't have time, or I don't have the money to play on Tour." When I left college, I never thought *if* I play on Tour, it was a matter of *when*. I made it happen. Money was definitely an issue, so I talked to a financial advisor and came up with a plan to set up an L.L.C. as a sponsorship vehicle. I was too busy working to train all the time, so I started to work in a health club to give myself the opportunity to train and play every day. **I made it happen. _You can too._** There are no permanent roadblocks and there is no reason you cannot accomplish whatever you decide you want to accomplish. More importantly, such a journey should be fulfilling. For me, it was my every thought and almost every day I looked forward to training and improving my level of play. That type of commitment to excellence is destined to be rewarding.

The caveat to all this is, **you must enjoy the journey.** I know that sounds cliché, but it is the absolute truth. It was not until recently that I really began to understand what that means. Before this realization, I drove myself harder and harder, blindly grinding away in pursuit of a dream. There were times that I would have been much better off taking time away from the game occasionally to live the rest of my life. I sacrificed time with loved ones, made injuries worse by not resting them, and reached a point of complete burn-out. I actually got to the point where I hated the game of Racquetball.

Please learn from my mistakes. If you are injured, take time off and let your body heal. If you are less than motivated or have the desire to do something else instead of playing a tournament, do so. There are plenty of tournaments every year, so you may not really miss

something irreplaceable. Remember, racquetball is a game, even if you are fortunate enough to do it for a living. Each moment should be savored and *lived*, not just glossed over. Enjoy the moment. Don't fall into the trap of expecting wins and hating your losses; learn from and enjoy both. They are equally important.

Each day, ask yourself this question... **"If I died tomorrow, would I be happy with the way I lived today?"** Are you putting your best effort into what is happening right now? Are you staying focused and doing the best you can at that given moment? If you are, then win or lose you can be proud of yourself and your efforts. That is how you find reward in what you do; not the trophies and checks, but rather in the satisfaction you get from learning to summon your talents at will, developing the personal discipline to prepare, and staying in top form most of the time. Those are the true rewards of being a competitive athlete. Don't sell yourself short. Don't ever think what you are doing is small-time. It is *your* big time and that is what matters.

> *"As you progress down the path, you may reach the point where you no longer just play the game. If you are persistent, you will begin to <u>understand</u> the game. When you continue down the path, and are diligent, you will move into Knowing."*
> *(Thomas McIntyre)*

> *"When you have achieved knowing, you will have access to all things; the ability to see the essence of everything."*
> *From the One thing, Know the ten thousand things.*
> *(Miymoto Musashi)*

"Minimalism is the key to greatness.
Efficiency is the key to success."
(Darrin Schenck)

Basic Philosophy:

In general terms, Racquetball is a simple game. There are six shots: Down the Line, Cross Court, Pinch, Splat, Serves and a Ceiling Ball -- that's it. If you attain mastery (9 out of 10 efficiency) over one of these shots, and are proficient at the others, you are a Pro player. If you are proficient (7 out of 10 efficiency) or better at two of these six, you are an Open player. The key to winning consistently is to structure your game around a solid game plan -- things that will work against every opponent you will face. This game plan will allow you to find ways to win even on those days when you are not playing your best. You <u>should</u> win when you're playing well, but can you still win on days when you're not having a peak experience? To quote Brad Gilbert (Career Grand Slam Tennis Champion Andre Agassi's former coach), "There are about five days a year when it seems no one on Earth could beat you, and there are five days a year where you couldn't beat my grandmother. The rest of the year is spent *somewhere* in the middle."

Since you will spend most of each year "*somewhere in the middle*", transferring the pressure to your opponent is critical. You can learn to beat people simply by hitting a decent lob serve, playing the proper court position and hitting the right shot. Those three things took me to a career high ranking of #18 in the world. **Percentage Racquetball** will win the majority of the time. Even when you are playing poorly, you can still execute some shots -- especially the easy ones. That is why you train and practice, to establish a <u>minimum</u> performance level. Whatever level you are on your **worst** day, is the level player you <u>really</u> are.

Changing Old Habits:

I know it is difficult to change swing mechanics and strategy after you have played the game for a while. It is best to take the view of starting a new habit versus changing an old one. As discussed in the book The Inner Game of Tennis, the author Tim Gallwey proposes this is a much better alternative because by changing an old habit, you are consciously starting the wrong way and fixing it. If you begin a new habit, it is correct from the start---once you get the hang of it. Trust me, the latter is much easier. In the area of footwork, it will take several stumbles and many incorrect steps before you begin to get it right. You must dedicate yourself and stick with your new techniques. You must be persistent, working on your own and/or with a partner to switch to this new technique. You must be willing to look foolish, trip over your own feet for awhile, and lose to players that you usually beat. This transition period will not be easy, but nothing that is worthwhile ever is. Halfway through the transition period is where most people give up and fall back into their old ways. This is why most people only improve by getting better at what they already do versus learning to play better racquetball. Don't give up; be willing to lose a few battles to win the war.

One magical day it will happen: *the breakthrough.* That is the day you have been waiting for. It may happen all at once, something will "click" and from that day forward you will be a better player. Progress will come bit by bit, but once you truly understand, a leap forward will take place. It is what makes all the work worthwhile. Players who in the past always beat you will now be struggling to keep up. People who do not understand how far you have progressed from the work you put in will rarely beat you. A breakthrough is a moment of enlightenment, a passage to a higher plane of existence on the court.

I attended the Elite Racquetball Training Camp at the Olympic Training Center in Colorado Springs. Dan Obremski was there as an instructor, and shared a great piece of advice. It was,

"Never be afraid to sacrifice who you are for what you might become." Dan went from being ranked in the high teens to a season-end top ten finish and a World Professional Championships title after cleaning up his life, committing himself to a better game plan on the court, and a more focused approach off the court. I think his statement is very true, in all aspects of life, not just racquetball. You should always be striving to improve the quality of your life, relationships, and the level of the pursuits you enjoy. Putting yourself and your ego at a reasonable amount of risk for growth in life is as necessary as weight training is for muscle growth.

"Winning is the science of total preparation."
(Joe Paterno, Penn State University Football Coach)

Equipment:

When you go to play in a tournament, **preparation is key**. You should have at least two racquets with exactly the same string and tension, preferably newly restrung, with the same size handles, and new grips. Also be sure to have two pairs of protective eyewear and court shoes that never see the outside world. Be sure to have new gloves, at least three or more if you perspire heavily. If you perspire a lot, wrist bands placed on the wrist of your racquet hand, but above the glove (not touching), will be helpful. Headbands or bandannas are a good idea. It's tough to see the ball with sweat running down the inside of your glasses. It's a good idea to have Ibuprofen handy, because you probably will need it sometime during the weekend. Always have a few balls on hand for warming up. A warm-up jacket is a must. Be sure to have enough clothing for each match on hand. Don't plan on wearing the same socks for back to back matches. Bring comfortable shoes to wear when you're not on the court.

If you are someone who cramps easily, be sure to have some potassium and calcium tablets handy and always be well hydrated. I always have some sort of meal replacement bar on hand because I may get hungry over the course of a long match. If I knew I was playing a few matches in a row, I would bring a cooler with a carbo-protein shake, a bagel or two and raisins, and I always had a gallon of water with me. I looked at tournaments as my job, and came prepared to spend the day functioning at as high a level as possible. If I took care of all those little things in advance, it was easier to focus on the task at hand.

The following is a checklist of the things I would routinely bring to a tournament:

Racquets

At least two of the same frame, same grip size. Newly restrung, but played with once to be sure the feel is OK. Be sure your grips are in good shape. If you play with the synthetic kind, you may want to replace them before each tournament.

Shoes

Get a decent pair of <u>racquetball</u> shoes. Cross trainers were not meant to grip a hardwood floor. Brand new shoes that you have never worn are bound to give you blisters, so bring shoes you are already comfortable with. Of course, you do not want to be competing in shoes that are about to fall to pieces. Broken down shoes offer inadequate support for all the running and stopping you will do over the course of a tournament.

Gloves

Have at least three good gloves with you. You are going to play matches frequently and they probably will not dry out between your matches. (especially if you go somewhere humid)

Be sure to have headbands and wristbands if you are a heavy sweater. I can play a whole tournament with the same glove, but my doubles partner changes gloves almost every game. Know thyself and come prepared!

Eyewear

You are required to wear them for tournament play, so obviously you will need at least one pair. I always like to have two on hand, just in case one pair gets broken or misplaced. My second pair has amber lenses in them in case I play on a court with a glass side wall.

Additional

I always carry some sort of topical analgesic, ibuprofen, medical tape, and extra shoe laces in my toiletry bag. I carry two sets of the string I like to use and one extra grip, just in case. I don't assume the club is going to provide shampoo, deodorant, etc. either, so I bring my own. All of this goes into my smaller club bag. If I am flying to a tournament, I also pack clothes in which to play my first match. Twice I have gone to tournaments and my luggage has been "lost" and I had to make do. Playing in someone else's shoes in no picnic.

Always have a warm-up ball or two, a jump rope, a jacket to wear to warm-up in (hence the name) and also to wear when you are done playing. Carry a pair of sandals or other comfortable shoes with you in case you have to stand and referee after your match.

Be sure to have meal replacement bars on hand to eat after you play. Avoid fast food like the plague. If the club has a snack bar, you may want to get a protein-carbo shake to help you recover from the rigors of your match. Bring money with you.

Make sure your have a lock and towel with you.

Pack all of your clothes into the large bag that you (should) have. It is much easier than jamming enough stuff for an entire weekend into one small bag or lugging around your big bag with all of your stuff in it. Make sure you bring enough clothes for an entire weekend of playing. You'll feel better in a new shirt and socks when you play back to back matches.

I always have a book and my Ipod with me. They provide good distractions when needed. Try to avoid getting bored, it's very draining.

Being a right-handed player,
this book is written from a right-handed
player's perspective.

The book also assumes you are <u>playing</u> a right-handed player. Please adjust accordingly if
necessary.

Classic errors to avoid

One of the greatest inhibitors of progress in racquetball is getting a good result from a bad swing. Most people who begin playing racquetball start by hacking around on a court somewhere with some friends. They have fun, get a good workout, and enjoy hitting the ball around the court. Herein lies the problem: most players do not take the time to learn how to play properly. The bad habits they are developing at this stage of the game are getting deeply ingrained with every swing. Some people become very accomplished players in spite of the lack of good fundamentals. Avoid copying a "unique" stroke from anyone. Proper instruction will save you years of frustration and heartache. How often do you hear someone who is a good golfer say they taught themselves how to play golf?

Another problem is if you walk around at a tournament, it is difficult to see players playing the game correctly; even most of the Open players are doing things the hard way. The average person cannot base their game on the principles that a very athletically gifted player. If you happen to be athletic, use that as a bonus, and not something to rely upon. If you are not, don't try to copy a style that is based on athletic ability, it just doesn't make sense. That is what I think is so much better about the system in this book, it works at every level. I do not teach things to a beginner any differently than I would an Open level player. **Percentage Racquetball** works relative to you and your opponent's ability. A beginning level player will not be able to cover the court or read the shots very well, but their opponent will not be hitting perfect passes either. The same is true on the other end of the spectrum. An Open level player should have good footwork and be able to cover a very good pass that another Open level player would be capable of hitting from the deep court. Most people play way too far forward. By playing this way, you are covering the tough shots and giving your opponent

the easy way out. Never make their job of winning easy. The reason this system works is because most players are doing things the hard way, and following this system will exploit that every time.

A third thing to remember is don't think it is ever too late...I didn't learn to play this way until I was already playing on the Pro Tour. I was willing to change my game and learn a more effective way of playing even at that point in my career. I would encourage everyone to take the same chance and improve your game, regardless of how long you have played.

An Overview of the Forehand Stroke:

Swing mechanics should be kept as simple as possible. The basic function of good mechanics is to execute a swing which is complimentary to your body. The swing starts in your feet and moves through your entire body, out your hand and into the shot. Leg drive and hip turn are important. Shoulder turn and wrist snap are critical. Timing is of the essence.

Again, minimalism is the key to greatness... Strive to develop only one swing for every single forehand you hit (ceiling balls and lob serves are excluded) and only one backhand swing. You should always adjust with your footwork and not your stroke. Your stroke should be the same mechanically regardless of your shot choice. The benefits of this are twofold:

One: In the interest of mechanical simplicity, learning one grip and one swing for every forehand and a separate one for the backhand is much easier than several variations of a stroke to get a desired shot. For example, if you open your stance to go cross court, that is one variation of the swing mechanics. To execute a down the line shot, you have to do something a little different mechanically. Altering your swing will increase your chance of making an error. If you always use the same swing mechanics and just alter your timing of that swing, you will increase the chances of hitting a good shot. Even if you mis-time the swing a little, you should still execute a good shot. It may not be the shot you wanted, but you are still in the rally.

Two: By using the same mechanics to hit all your shots, you are giving your opponent very little information to read and anticipate your shot. This will freeze them in place and force them to <u>react</u> to your shot, rather than allowing them to read your shots and leaning the right direction. By freezing your opponent in position, you will always have shots with which to

win a rally, if you execute them correctly. Very few players will cover the court effectively, so there are ample opportunities to win rallies. Court coverage and shot selection will be covered later.

When you learn to use good mechanics to hit the ball, you will experience less wear and tear on your body, hit the ball harder and stay more consistent over the course of a match. If you are hitting the ball crisply with all arm on Friday of a tournament, by Saturday afternoon your arm is likely to resemble a noodle, which is definitely not conducive to being consistent or winning tournaments. If your strategy and shots change throughout a weekend or even over the course of a match, if you constantly tax your body and cannot do things at 5-5 in the tie-breaker that you can do at 5-5 in the first game, you will be spinning your wheels.

知识就是力量

Knowledge is Power

The Forehand Grip:

To grip the racquet properly, hold it in your left hand so it is perpendicular to the floor. Now with your right hand, "shake hands" with the handle of the racquet. The "V" that your thumb and finger make should go up the frame of the racquet as illustrated. Be sure that your little finger is at least on the bottom of the handle. **All forehands are hit with this grip, period.**

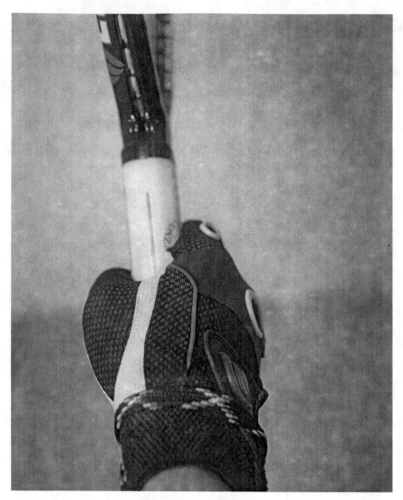

The Correct Forehand Grip

This version of the grip will give you much more margin for error. The proper stroke will mean that your racquet is perpendicular to the floor throughout your hitting zone. The timing needs to be good, but not perfect to work. Again, building margin for error into your game is the essence of this book.

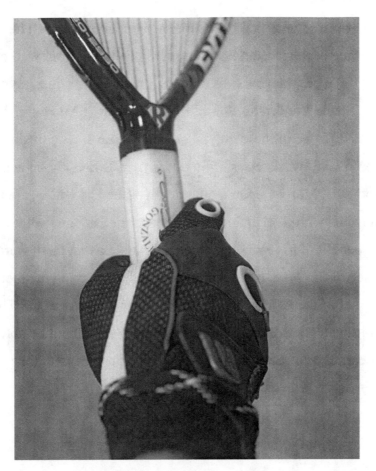

The more difficult version.

In the previous picture, my racquet is perpendicular to the floor. In the above picture, the sweet spot is pointing towards the floor. Which do you think has more margin for error?

Some players use a grip similar to that of holding a hammer or a club. The problem with the club grip is that the face of the racquet is only squared up to the front wall outside the normal hitting zone. Some of the best players ever hold their racquet like this; guys like Cliff Swain, Kane Waselenchuk, Shane Vanderson, John Ellis, and others. I hate to be the one to point this out, but you are NOT one of these guys. *You* will end up slicing the ball most of the time. What these players do takes world class timing. It is very difficult to be consistent with this grip. In the 70's and 80's, Marty Hogan inadvertently ruined an entire generation of players because he hit forehands with a backhand grip. Players tried to copy what Marty did, but without having the benefit of his amazing athletic ability to assist them were bound to struggle. The essence of this book is teaching you a method playing racquetball that allows room for error. Neither of these grips gives you any room for error at all. The grip is absolutely key to hitting a good shot. If your grip is off, you will not be able to execute the shots you desire. Learn the correct grip; the proper swing begins with the proper grip.

If you have specific questions,
visit rbguru.com

Commentary on the "old school" swing.

It was a common thought in racquetball to have a pendulum type swing, contacting the ball just above the floor. There are several problems with this type of swing:

1. It leaves you no room whatsoever for error. If you mis-time the shot even a tiny bit, you either hit it into the floor or sail it much higher than intended.
2. It is hard on the arm and lower back. Most players who swing this way bend at the waist, which is hard on the lower back muscles. This swing is putting most of the stress on the arm only, not allowing you to use the rest of your body for the swing.
3. The mechanics of your stroke has to change to hit certain shots. A cross court shot will be all wrist and splats are very difficult to hit this way.

Do not bend at the waist; it is hard on the lower back
and disrupts your mechanics.

With these things in mind, let's move on to the proper swing.

It is not daily increase, but daily decrease.
Hack away the unessential.
--Bruce Lee

The Forehand swing.

The swing starts with your knees slightly bent and a stride parallel to the side wall, toward the front wall. You want the ball to be just short of an arm and racquet length away from the body, and ideally contact the ball about knee high. Get your racquet back early, elbow as high as the shoulder. Do not lock your elbow, bend it just a little to attain the fullest amount of leverage without damaging or fatiguing the arm. After striding towards the front wall, plant your left foot, start the swing with your <u>left elbow</u>, pulling with your back muscles and shoulders. Be sure your spine stays as straight as possible to allow optimum rotation and minimum stress on the body. Now rotate your hips into the shot, as you continue to swing with your shoulders and now the right arm. Your eyes should be locked onto the ball as early as possible and throughout the stroke. The last thing you do is snap the wrist at impact. Your weight should stay balanced and distributed equally between your feet. A big follow through is important, ensuring that you accelerate <u>through</u> the shot. Do not attempt to stop your swing, allow your body to do that for you. If you stop the swing short, you will lose power <u>and</u> accuracy.

This is the proper starting position for the forehand. My elbow is as high as my shoulder, my racquet up and parallel to the side wall. My feet, hips and shoulders are all parallel to the side wall.

In this picture, I have pulled with my shoulders, turned my hips, and kept my eyes on the ball. I am contacting the ball in the exact middle of my stance to execute a straight in shot. Be sure to bend your knees, even on the shots that are a little high in your hitting zone. Balance and contact point are critical. Regardless of its height, the shot is still dictated by the contact point in relation to your feet. Even an overhead hit in line with your front foot will go cross court. **This is why footwork is so critical; your hitting zone is dictated by your feet.** If you don't get them in position, it will be difficult to hit shots consistently. Be sure that you follow through but stay the same height that you began your swing. If you rise up as you finish, the shot will rise up as well.

Stay level during your follow through. I finish my swing level, balanced,
and with my torso now facing the front wall.

There is a fine line between posing in your follow-through and charging back into court position. You must finish the shot but not stand there and watch what happens. Work at hustling back into good court position after hitting the shot, just as much as you hustled to the shot your opponent just hit. Commit to the shot; hit it,......and then recover to good court position in anticipation of your opponent retrieving the shot you've just hit. Don't get stuck out of position by swinging and standing in that spot to assess what is happening. Be sure not to run out of your shot before you are finished swinging, either. You must study this diligently.

The point of contact dictates where the ball will go...timing is what changes your shots. **The stroke should always be the same.** If you contact the ball early in your stance (just inside your front foot), it will go cross court. If you contact the ball deep in your stance, (just in front of your back foot) you will hit a splat. That is how you *should* execute those shots. If you rely on wrist snap or turning your body to hit a cross court shot or a splat, it will be more difficult to achieve consistency. You will be giving your opponent information as to where you are hitting your next shot if you contact the ball in the middle of your stance and turn you feet. That means you now have to hit a better shot to win because your opponent knows where the ball is going and will be headed that direction as soon as you begin your swing.

Proper Contact Point for the Cross Court

Always strive to contact the ball about knee high. If you let the ball drop to shoe top level, you will have to bend at the waist to hit the shot. This will change your mechanics and therefore increase the chances of making an error. You have literally no room for error by attempting to make the ball travel two inches above the floor. As discussed before, bending at the waist not only is hard on the body, it is not conducive to being consistent.

Proper Contact point for the Down the Line

I used the dotted line to illustrate the middle of my stance
as the proper contact point for a down the line shot.

**If you have specific questions,
visit rbguru.com**

Proper Contact Point for the Pinch or Splat

Again, I used the dotted line to reference the middle of my stance.
A splat should be contacted just inside the back foot..

All of the forehands you hit are with the same stroke; the only variable is where you contact the ball in relation to your feet. By changing the timing of your swing, you execute the different shots. This has a twofold benefit: It is simpler for you to execute and it forces your opponent to react your shot vs. anticipate what you are about to do.

Section Summary---the Forehand

--Be sure your grip is correct.

--Get the racquet back early. Early racquet preparation is essential to the execution of all of your shots.

--Feet parallel to the side wall. Start with your knees bent slightly.

--Step toward the front wall.

--The swing begins with your left elbow, pulling the rest of your upper body through the hitting zone.

--Snap your hips into the shot.

--Eyes on the ball until contact. Snap wrist at impact.

--Contact the ball knee high.

--Be sure to follow all the way through, accelerating through your hitting zone and beyond. Let you body stop your swing, not your arm.

--Good balance and proper footwork **increase power and consistency.**

The Backhand

The Backhand Grip

Beginning from a forehand grip, turn the racquet slightly towards the palm of your right hand. Please note in the picture that the seam in my glove is just slightly behind the grip itself. This keeps my racquet parallel to the floor throughout my hitting zone.

Correct Backhand Grip

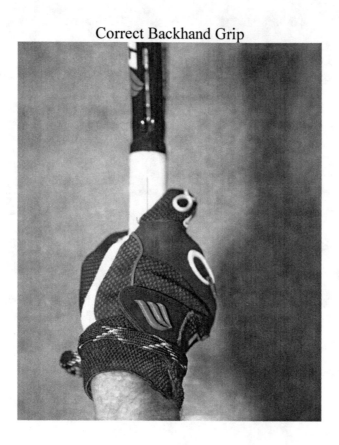

Too far over!

You must learn to correctly switch grips on the fly. You do not have time during a rally to look at your hand to see if your grip is right, so practice so you can do it by feel alone.

The problems with the grip that is too far over are that it forces you to time your stroke perfectly, leaves you no room for error, and also makes you contact the ball out in front of your stance. This typically puts more wear and tear on your arm.

The Backhand Stroke

The backhand stroke starts again with your eyes on the ball, keeping them focused on the ball until impact. The swing begins with your right foot stepping at a 45 degree angle into the shot. Racquet back early, and keep it away from your body. Be sure that you are more than an arm and racquet length away from the ball, not locking the elbow. You want to stride into the ball at 45 degrees, so you need to allow yourself enough room to execute the shot. **Be sure to contact the ball as close to knee high as possible. This will leave you some margin for error.** After planting your right foot, begin the stroke by pulling with your back muscles on the right side of your body. Add the shoulders into the swing, and now rotate the hips through. Be sure to pull with your shoulders, not push with your thumb. The backhand should feel as if it is one-third back swing and two-thirds follow through. This is because the racquet is on the side of your body facing the front wall, versus the forehand where it is behind your body. If you turn too far back on your back swing, you will lose sight of the ball.

Your weight should finish on your right foot, without leaning forward. Get low with your legs first, and then stride into the ball at the same height established by the knee bend. *Do not get low by bending at the waist.* This will limit your rotation and change the path of your shoulders and consequently your racquet. Also, do not go down as you strike the ball, it is too difficult to time this perfectly every time. If you bend as you hit the ball, you are likely to hit the shot into the floor.

The hitting zone for the backhand is similar to the forehand. The contact point dictates where the ball will go. If you contact the ball even with the outside edge of your front foot, this will make the ball go down the line...Earlier contact will result in a cross court, and a shot contacted behind the front foot will hit a splat.

Note my racquet is back early; bend your knees in advance.

Eyes on the ball early, and keep watching the ball until
it is hit by your racquet.

Finish with a big follow through and stay
level throughout the swing.

Additionally...

You can tell if you are executing the swing properly in several ways. One is to go by the feel of it. The body knows when it does something mechanically correct and you will feel the difference. Almost every student I have ever worked with could tell when they hit a shot employing good mechanics. The right swing will feel effortless and smooth, yet utilizes the power generated much more efficiently. It is like a good golf swing in that if you do it once, you will yearn for more.

Another way to tell is by the sound. When you slice, chop or do not make solid, flat contact with the ball, you can hear the sound it makes. When you do it correctly, it makes two noises, one when it hits the racquet and one when it hits the front wall. It will sound like a "kaa-bang" when you do it right. Don't worry, you'll know it when you do it.

Section Summary---the Backhand

--**Be sure your grip is correct.**

-- **Racquet back early.**

--**Step at a 45 degree angle (towards the left front corner).**

--**Be sure to start with a slight knee bend.**

-- **Swing starts with the right shoulder, which pulls the rest of the upper**

      body through the hitting zone.

--**Turn your hips into the shot.**

--**Shift your weight forward into the shot.**

--**Contact the ball knee high.**

--**Eyes on the ball until contact.**

-- **Big follow-through.**

--**Stay level throughout the swing.**

Serves

You must take advantage of the serve as often as possible. Your sole purpose for entering the service box is to score points, so be sure to carefully consider what you are about to do. You must become proficient at remembering what is working, what is not, and what you have yet to try. Remember that a person's weakness usually gets weaker as the match goes on. So if you tried a serve the first game and did well with it, you may want to go back to it in the tie-breaker. Develop the capacity to remember and use the information you gather over the course of a match. Even though it may appear that some of the Pros walk into the service box and casually hit a serve into play, the intent is to limit their opponent's options by hitting a serve they know has worked in the past. **When in doubt, start with <u>your</u> best serve and see how it works.** If they handle it well, move on down your list of serves until you find something that works. Remember that when you find one serve that works, keep searching for at least one other.

Serving first in racquetball is not as critical as it is in tennis. But, there are some advantages to getting in the service box first. Here are three reasons why I like to serve first:

1. Your opponent may be a slow starter.

Many players like to "play their way into a match". Those are the same people who show up at the club, hit a few balls and jump right onto the challenge court. It takes a while for them to get up to full speed. If you can jump out to a 5-0 lead or better, it

will put a lot of pressure on your opponent to hit good shots to catch up to you. This quickly can deter some opponents.

2. You may be on fire to start out.

Preparation is key. After a good warm up, you may come out firing and hit a lot of good serves and shots right from the start. Again, this will put pressure on your opponent. I have seen plenty of matches that were all but over by the middle of the first game.

3. Your opponent may be nervous at the start of the match.

Many players are too "amped up" when they begin a match and will take bad shots, make bad decisions, skip balls or leave shots up. A lot of people over-swing when they are nervous. You can capitalize on this. It takes most players until the middle of the first game to settle into the match and get comfortable. This may give you the opportunity to build a lead to start the match.

Winning the first game greatly increases your chances of winning the match.

知识就是力量

Knowledge is Power

The Lob Serve

OK, here we go...time to put some points on the board. You're in the service box, ball in your hand and can hit any serve you want. Be sure to have a clear picture in your mind before you start your motion. Do not begin your motion and "choose on the fly," thinking this will keep your opponent guessing. Instead, you will be less accurate than you could be, and precision is key to the lob serve. Take your time, decide what you want to do, picture it in your mind, and then do it.

You have many choices, so let's start with the serves hit from the right side of the box and continue from there. Bear in mind, all the lob serves are hit with the feet square to the side wall unless otherwise noted. All serves should be hit from about six feet from the right side wall. Take a small step forward as part of your motion. To improve your accuracy and consistency, watch the ball hit the strings of your racquet instead of looking at your target. **Think about your target but *watch* the ball.**

Most of your lob serves will be hit from this starting position. Exceptions are noted in the text. Half lobs can use the same beginning position if you wish.

Half lob to the backhand.

This is a good serve to hit in several situations. One, if your opponent is being very aggressive and trying to cut the serve off, a good half lob can neutralize this attempt or, at least, force them to make difficult shots to win the rally. Two, it is easy to disguise, allowing you to hit half lobs to the forehand and backhand side to keep your opponent off balance and make them arrive to the ball later than they would prefer. Three, by altering the serve slightly, it can be an effective serve to the deep court.

The half lob serve to the backhand is executed by standing one step to the right of the center of the service box. This will allow you to get into good court position as soon as possible. Start with your racquet up and your elbow just off your right hip. Aim about 10 feet high and dead center on the front wall. Bounce (don't just drop) the ball, so it rebounds up to chest high and "push" the ball cross court so it bounces just past the short line. This placement is important...if you hit the ball too close to the five foot line, it is much easier for your opponent to cut-off the serve.

Note that my eyes are on the ball at contact; my shoulders are turning
in order to execute the serve.

Execute this serve by locking your wrist in place and just turning your shoulders into the ball. This is one big, easy movement instead of a small, fine move like a wrist snap or a slice, which can break down more easily under pressure. Be sure to bounce the ball forward in your stance, so you can continue the ball's direction instead of dropping the ball in the middle of your stance and snapping your wrist to get the ball cross court. You want the ball to bounce just beyond the service line because it will be above your opponent's waist by the time he can play the shot. That will minimize his chances of hitting a killshot in front of you. The five foot line rule will keep your opponent out of that zone until the ball hits the floor and is well on its way up. This means the response will probably be a cross court pass coming to you in your good court position. You have the option of shooting the ball or going to the ceiling and waiting for a better opportunity. Another version of this serve is to bounce the ball above your head and hit a soft overhead, basically pushing the ball cross court to the backhand side. This adds a little more height to the half lob; very effective against shorter players and/or players who do not hit the ball well from high in their hitting zone.

Half Lob to the Forehand

A half lob to the forehand should be basically the same thing as a half lob to the backhand, except your target should be a little higher. Be sure to bounce the ball in the middle of your stance and "push" it about 15 feet high on the front wall. Strive to make the ball go up after hitting the front wall. Hit it so it bounces just behind the short line. Again, this placement is critical, especially when serving to most players' forehands. They will tend to be more aggressive and attack a serve to this side. Get into good court position as soon as possible because the easiest shot for your opponent to hit off of this serve is to hammer the ball cross court. If you are not in position, you will be scrambling to retrieve the first shot of the rally. This negates the advantage you had in being the server.

See photos on the following pages.

Half Lob to the Forehand

You can see in relation to the sticker on the front wall that this serve is going to hit about 12' off the floor. This will make the ball bounce just behind the 5 foot line, and be high in your opponent's hitting zone. This usually forces a cross court, or makes any other shot much more difficult.

A word of caution…

Do not get sucked into being aggressive with every return your opponent hits. Be smart and wait for good opportunities to score points. Don't take yourself out of the service box by forcing shots and taking low percentage shots. Be patient.

High Lob to the Backhand

Since many players attack every lob serve that is hit, a lot of players have stopped serving a high lob straight to the left corner. The main thing to consider is whether or not you are getting opportunities off of this serve. Most people do not like it when someone cuts off their serve, but whether or not it is comfortable is irrelevant. Can you get used to scoring points? Well, then you can tolerate someone cutting off your serves.

This serve is executed by starting with the racquet back, bouncing the ball approximately chest high and lifting the shot up towards the center of the front wall, about six feet below the ceiling. The ball should go up after hitting the front wall. The ball should land on the five foot line and carry to the left corner. It should hit low enough on the back wall so that your opponent has only a splat or no shot at all from this position.

If your opponent plays the ball from deep court, he should have limited choices and this plays right into your good court position. If they decide to cut the serve off, the ball must be short-hopped to avoid breaking the plane of the five foot line. This is difficult for some players. The most likely returns are cross court and a splat, so be ready to capitalize on these chances. These shots will come right into your good court position.

***Keep in mind the reason a lot of people quit hitting this serve is because many players got better at cutting the ball off. Hit a few of these serves and find out whether or not your opponent can effectively attack this serve. Use this serve accordingly.

High Lob to the Backhand—contact point

High lob to the Backhand

Note where the ball contacts the front wall to execute this serve. The ball so travel <u>upwards</u> after contacting the front wall. This puts the proper arch on the serve

High Lob to the Forehand

In spite of the high lob to the backhand going "out of style," the high lob to the forehand is still a very common serve. In fact, I don't think people serve to their opponent's forehand often enough. Most players will take more risks and therefore make more errors on this side. Don't be afraid to serve this side. It may give you more chances to win points than you think.

This serve should be hit by starting with your racquet back, bouncing the ball up to chest high and pushing it up to the front wall about six feet from the ceiling. The ball should go up after contacting the front wall. Strive to land the ball on the five foot line or slightly deeper, so your opponent has to play the ball deeper in the court. Square your feet to the side wall and bounce the ball halfway between where you would contact a splat and a down the line shot. If done correctly, the ball will hit the front wall about three feet from the side wall and get closer to the side wall the deeper into the court it goes. Do not try to "roll" the ball down the side wall; it is too hard to do repeatedly, especially under pressure.

As with the others, the starting position and the contact look the same.

High lob to the Forehand

A good high follow through is necessary on all lob serves. Strive to hit these with a big, smooth motion to promote consistency.

Lob Z to the Forehand

Another good serve to hit to someone who is aggressive with the return is to hit a High Lob Z to the Forehand. The easiest response to this serve is to smash the ball cross court, which is right to you, if you can get set in time. Again, don't get sucked into taking a bad shot from this position. Don't get caught running backwards and trying to kill the ball; it's way too hard to do this consistently. Go to the ceiling and wait for a better opportunity. If you are getting good opportunities, such as when your opponent tries to hit a splat or sails a cross court off the back wall, then stick with it. Here's how:

Open your stance slightly (left foot moved to the left) and bounce the ball chest high. Start with your racquet back and begin your motion by turning your shoulders and lifting the ball up to the left corner. Obviously the ball must hit the front wall first, so aim about three feet away from the side wall and three feet below the ceiling. The ball will carry into the side wall and come toward you. Be sure the ball goes in front of you, not behind you. According to the rules, you must stay in the service box until the ball crosses the short line, but you can move to your left inside the box after hitting the serve and give yourself a better chance of getting to the proper court position after the ball crosses the short line. Move left and make sure the ball passes in front of you. Get ready for your opponent to cut the ball off and hit an overhead

shot. Take notice if they really square up to the side wall; this is a good sign they may try to

go down the line. Be ready to cover this shot, as well as a cross court.

If the serve is not cut off, it should bounce just behind the five foot line and hit the side wall first in the deep court, striking very low on the back wall. The serve should hit the side wall about two feet from the back wall so that the only return your opponent should have is a splat.

Lob Nick to the Backhand

The purpose of this serve is to pin your opponent in the middle of the deep court and cut down their angles to get the ball around you.

To execute this serve, start in the same place you have for the previous serves. Start with your racquet back, bounce the ball even with your front foot and up to chest high. Your racquet should come from just below shoulder level around to the ball and slightly upward. Develop the feel of "brushing" across the ball without really slicing it. You want the ball to hit just right of center and carry deep into the left side wall about four feet high. An ideal lob nick will hit the side wall on the fly, bounce and travel towards the door provided the door is in the middle of the court. A perfect one will hit the door handle.

When done properly, this serve will be difficult to cut off due to the height before it strikes the side wall, and is difficult to short-hop off the floor. If hit properly, the ball will carry to the door (middle of the court) which minimizes the angle to hit a pass. Your opponent will have to take the ball out of the air just after hitting the side wall or hope it comes off the back wall. It is a great serve when correctly executed. It plays right into the court position you will be using because most players think the easiest shot to hit off this serve is a splat.

Lob Nick to the Backhand

Note the same high follow through as I finish

Lob Nick to the Forehand

This serve is easier to execute if you are standing on the far left side of the service box. Close your stance so that your left foot is out much farther than the right Start with your racquet back, bounce the ball even with your back foot and make contact with it chest high. You are aiming five feet below the ceiling, and about five feet to eight feet away from the side wall. Use a good shoulder turn, not a wrist snap to execute this serve. The racquet should brush the ball and again it should go up after hitting the front wall. The ball should hit the right wall halfway between the five foot line and the back wall at about chest high. A perfect lob nick will hit the door handle if you do it correctly. (Assuming the door is in the middle of the court.)

Be sure you close your stance a little for this serve. If you put your left foot ahead of your right foot, and drop the ball in the middle of your stance, you should get the correct angle for this serve. See example below for the right foot position.

知识就是力量

Knowledge is Power

Lob Nick to the Forehand

This is a good serve to hit to a Lefties backhand, but also a good serve to hit to Righties as well. Most players will take more chances on there forehand, and therefore may make more errors on that side.

Lob Z to the Backhand

This serve should also be hit from the left side of the service box. I prefer to hit this serve with my backhand, because it will make it easier to get into good position after the serve. Start with your racquet back and your feet set up for a back hand facing the right corner. Bounce the ball a little lower this time and lift the serve up to the front wall about three feet from the side wall. It should hit the side wall and come right back toward you, so move to the right and get out of the way. Be sure this Z serve also goes in front of you, not behind you. Get the ball to bounce inside the five foot line and carry toward the left side wall. If your opponent cuts this serve off, it will probably go cross court because that is the easiest angle for them to hit.

***Be sure when you hit this serve that you are moving to your right after you contact the ball. You want to make sure the ball passes in front of you just before it crosses the service line. If the ball goes behind you, you're either going to get beat by a cross court pass, or an ugly ball mark. (Please send a picture of the ball mark to my website at www.rbguru.com for all posterity to view :-) You want to be in position to cover the cross court anyway, so get moving that direction early.

Your starting position should look like this: ball in hand and racquet back. Drop the ball and follow through as shown in the second picture.

Big follow through on this serve as well.

Section Summary--- the Lob Serves

--Decide ahead of time and picture in your mind what serve you are going

to hit.

--Pick your starting position and take a small step towards the front wall.

--Limit your motion to big, smooth movements. Avoid short, choppy

movements. Never slice the ball.

--Watch the ball until the racquet contacts it.

--Get back into position as soon as the ball crosses the short line.

--Keep track of your success with each serve. If you find one that works,

be sure to find at least one more that you can also score

points with.

-- Be sure to try a variety of serves and continue to use the ones

you have success with.

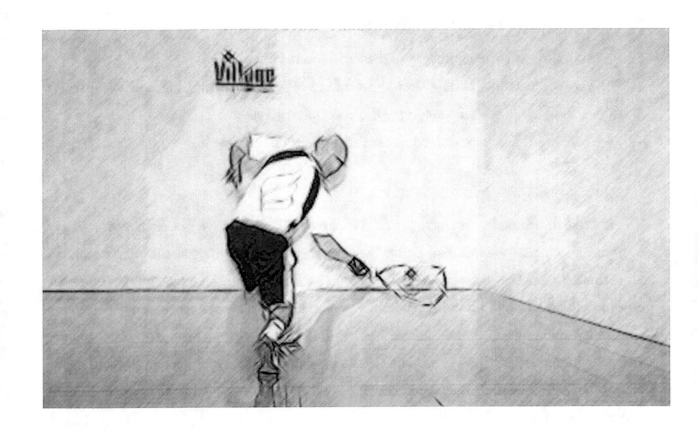

Drive Serves

A couple of things to keep in mind about the drive serve:

1   It is hard work generating your own power on every serve.

2   You will usually not have time to get into ideal position after hitting a drive serve.

3   A short serve is a side out in the Pro and Open division.

4   A serve off the back wall could be a set up for your opponent.

But, it's not all bad news. In fact, a good drive serve will be effective against almost everyone you face. By aiming the ball at the corners, the serves will have different results. Sometimes the serve will bounce and then hit the back wall first, shooting straight out. Other times it will bounce and hit the side wall first, coming into your opponent's body. This gives you some "randomness" to that same serve. It will keep your opponent guessing and set up the rest of your serves. Cheap points and easy first shots are always welcome, and will make your job of scoring easier if you can execute a good drive serve on command. So, let's move into the drive serve.

I recommend beginning the drive serve motion from the same place you would begin most of your lob serve. This is to again facilitate getting into the proper court position as the rally begins. Begin your serve from the right side of the service box, one medium step out of the middle. Start with both feet on the short line of the service box, right foot in back of your left and about two shoe lengths apart. The motion begins with a step with the right foot towards the front wall, then bounce the ball, then a stride with the left foot. Your feet should end up parallel to the side wall when the steps are completed. The racquet comes up as soon as you drop the ball and the swing starts by pulling with your left elbow. When you plant that left foot, you must learn to snap your hips into the shot. Strive to bounce the ball into the same hitting zone you would for a forehand. The motion is exactly the same as a forehand hit during the rally. By adding a good shoulder turn, wrist snap, and a big follow-through, you have yourself a Drive serve. Remember to watch the ball until it leaves your strings. You will move the ball around the court by changing the place you drop the ball, thereby changing the contact point for each serve.

This is the correct starting position for the Drive Serve.

知识就是力量

Knowledge is Power

Your service motion should remain the same for almost every drive serve. **This is the best way to fool your opponent: make all the serves look the same**. If you "head fake" or step one way and hit the other, your are going to be less consistent mechanically and therefore not as effective. You are also giving your opponent something to look for the next time you hit that serve. Even if you look one way and hit another, you are still giving clues as to where the serve will go. For a Drive Z to the Backhand of a right-handed player, you will need to change not only the motion, but also the place from which you serve.

A good drive serve to the backhand will hit the floor about half way between the short line and the five foot line. Don't aim for an inch over the line; you will most likely hit too many short serves. Remember---room for error is critical to consistency. If you hit the ball higher and it travels into the corner, a good angle will help the serve to still be effective. If you do happen to hit the ball a little too low, then you have some room for it to clear the serve line. Keep in mind that you must have a clear picture in your head of what serve you are going to hit. If you change your mind once you start your motion, it is likely that you will not hit a good serve. The mind and body do not work well with general ideas. You must be as specific as possible with your thought process to get the desired result.

The following picture is the contact point for the drive serve to the backhand corner. I am about 5'8", but my stride still covers most of the service box. Contact the forward in your stance to make the ball to go cross court.

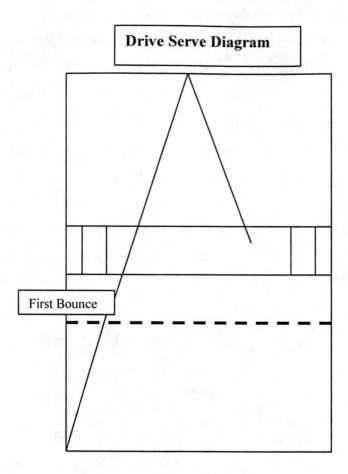

Drive Serve Diagram

First Bounce

As I had stated before, you are aiming to the corner to add some "randomness" to the serve. Vary the height and speed to further change the appearance of this serve.

Jam Serve

A good Jam Serve will begin the exact same way the drive serve to the left corner and should look exactly the same all the way through. The only difference in this serve is that you will drop the ball a little farther forward in your stance than a serve which will travel to the left corner. The idea is to get the ball to hit the side wall about even with the five foot line and come directly at your opponent. This serve should be hit between knee and waist high into the side wall. The serve should jam your opponent, hence the name, and force them into "fighting off" the shot for an uncomfortable position. There are very few players who have the presence of mind to square around and hit a forehand off of this serve. By trying to hit a backhand which is closer to the body than they would like, it is highly likely your opponent will make an error and/or give you an opportunity. It is a great serve to mix in and a good choice in a tight situation when you need to score a point without the risk of a short serve.

Please refer to the next picture.

The Jam Serve

The Jam serve and the Wrap around serve look very similar, but should be two separate serves. One comes right at your opponent, and the other goes behind them and wraps around to the forehand.

The Jam Serve Diagram

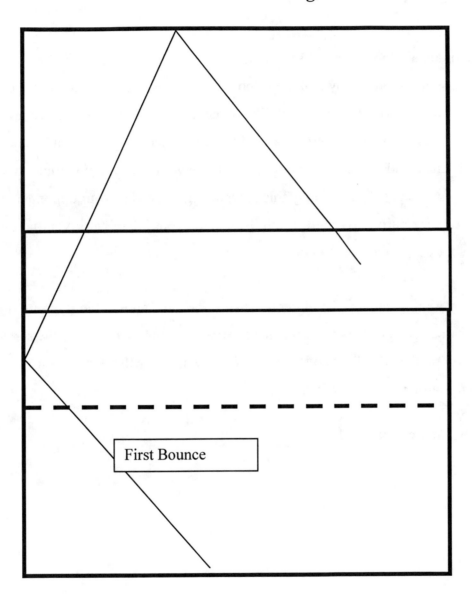

First Bounce

The Wrap-around Serve

This serve should again look exactly like the drive serve to the left corner. The effectiveness of the serve is greatly improved by making it look like the other serves and therefore not allowing your opponent to get a jump on it. The object of this serve is to force your opponent to either short hop the serve with their backhand before the back wall, or let it go and chase to ball to the forehand side. The second bounce of the serve should end up around the five foot line on the forehand side. It is likely this serve will get ahead of your opponent and they will have to hit their return cross court. Provided you did your job of getting into proper court position, this shot will come right to you.

Hit this serve by aiming about waist high on the side wall, and around the five foot line. Hit this serve the same speed as the rest of the drive serves. Be sure to get out of the service box and into position on the **LEFT** side of the court, otherwise you will be in the way of the serve as it comes around to the forehand side.

Please refer to the next photo.

Wrap Around Serve

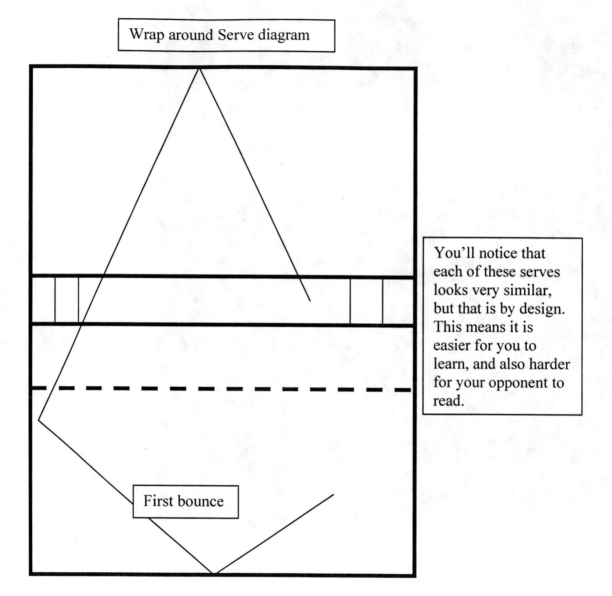

Wrap around Serve diagram

You'll notice that each of these serves looks very similar, but that is by design. This means it is easier for you to learn, and also harder for your opponent to read.

First bounce

The objective of this serve is to force your opponent to spin and then chase the ball to the forehand side.

The Drive Z to the Forehand

From the same position in the box and with the same service motion, drop the ball farther in front of your left foot and snap your wrist. This serve should be hit as high as the jam and wrap-around serves. If it is too low, it will not reach it's desired location in the court. The Drive Z should cross the short line at about waist high. The angle should be tight in the corner, about two and a half to three and a half feet (which is two racquet lengths) from the side wall. The serve should strike the front wall and then the side wall, travel behind you, and then bounce behind the five foot line and hit the opposite side wall within two feet of the back wall. The ball should travel parallel to the back wall if it is done correctly which limits the receiver's choices as to what return to hit. If the serve is too shallow or too deep, it is not very effective. A good Drive Z serve will hit the right side wall and kick straight out toward the receiver. If done properly, there is no room for the receiver to get his racquet behind the ball and hit a good shot. You want to disguise this serve by making it look the same as all the over serves. You do not want someone to cut off your Z serve before it gets to the side wall.

Please refer to the next picture

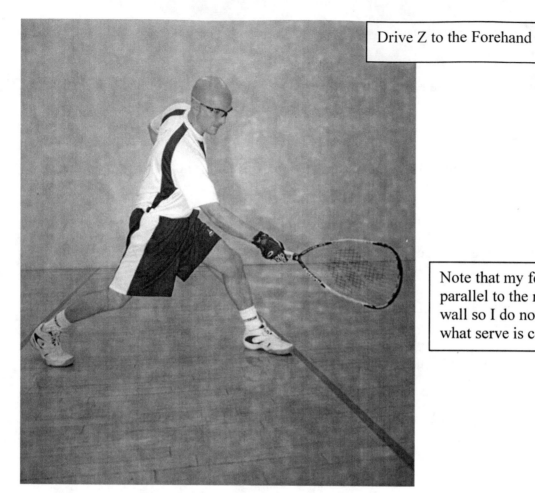

Drive Z to the Forehand

Note that my feet are still parallel to the right side wall so I do not give away what serve is coming.

This serve should be hit slightly upwards, so that it is about chest high when it gets to the right corner of the court.

Diagram for the Drive Z to the Forehand

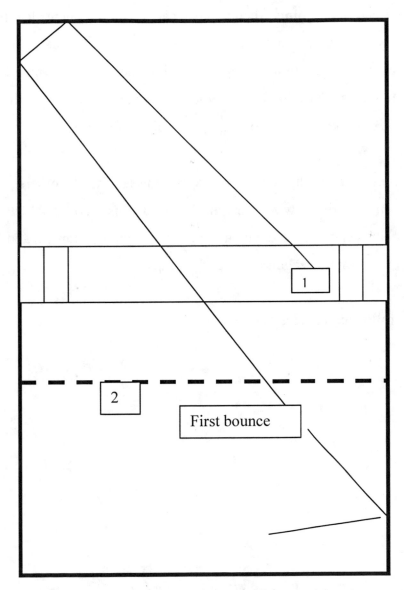

I know, it doesn't really look like a Z. Start the serve from position 1.

Be sure you get back into position 2 and get out of the way of the return.

Drive Serve to the Forehand

This serve is a good way score points when you can catch your opponents leaning towards the backhand side trying to get a jump on those serves. After properly executing this serve a few times, you force your opponent to respect both sides, and thereby giving you more room to get your serves to the backhand in. Even if you hit this serve short, you still get your opponent thinking about defending this one as well as all the others.

Again, you are striving to make this serve look exactly the same as the others. Don't head fake, step away, or in any other way alter the mechanics on this serve. "Sell" this serve by making it look just like everything else you are throwing at your opponent, and force them to react to it instead of reading it and getting an early jump on it.

Please refer to the following pictures and diagram.

知识就是力量

Knowledge is Power

Contact point for the Drive serve to the forehand.

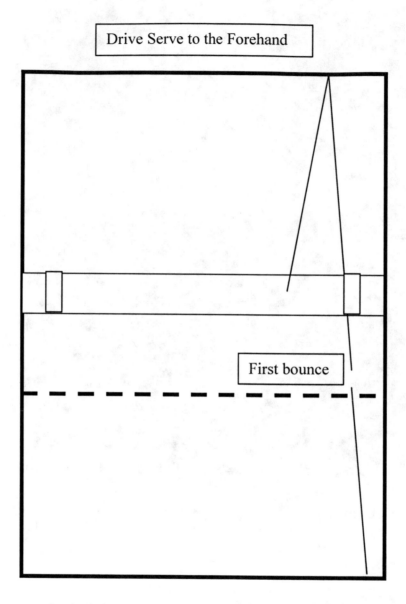

Drive Serve to the Forehand

First bounce

This serve travels the shortest distance, so you should contact the ball a little lower so it is less likely to come off the back wall.

The Drive Z to the Backhand

This serve is hit from the far left side of the service box. You will start with your feet facing the right corner, and will step that direction after you drop the ball. This serve should again be hit higher than all the other drive serves. Drop the ball and swing slightly upwards toward the right corner. Hit the front wall about two to three and a half feet away from the side wall, then it will strike the side wall. Make the serve bounce behind the five foot line. Like the Z to the Forehand, it should hit the left side wall about two feet from the back wall and kick straight out towards the receiver parallel to the back wall. A good Z serve will give your opponent very few choices of what return to hit. This serve is difficult to cut off and hit down the line because of the angle at which it comes to the receiver. Hit the serve and get into good court position because the shot is most likely coming into that zone.

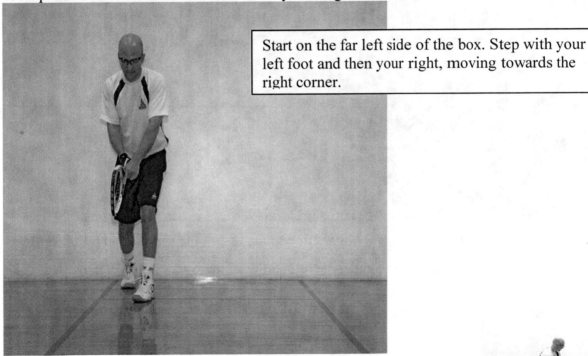

Start on the far left side of the box. Step with your left foot and then your right, moving towards the right corner.

This serve should be contacted higher in relation to the rest of the serves, and hit upwards so it rises as it travels to the left corner of the back court.

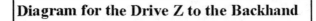

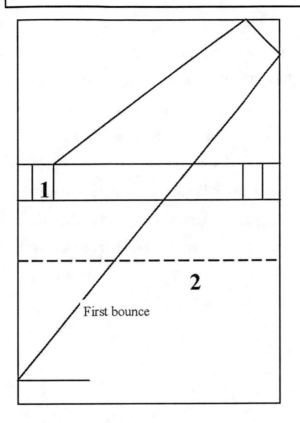
Diagram for the Drive Z to the Backhand

1

2

First bounce

This is one of the few serves you will hit that you are going to "telegraph" where you are going to serve. Commit to the serve and hit it, there is not much your opponent can do to a good Z serve.

After serving the Z, turn and follow the ball while you get back into position. Start your serve from position 1 and get to position 2 as soon as possible.

Chest High Drive Z to the Backhand

This is a variation of the Drive Z to the backhand. It is begun from the same place in the box, the far left side. Bounce the ball back up to chest high and hit the ball about eye level into the right corner. The serve should do the same thing as a regular Drive Z, except it will be chest high when it gets to your opponent. This will be more difficult for them to cut off, so it is a good serve to hit to someone who is always trying to cut off the Drive Z. This should make them play the angle of the serve from deep court, or at least make the cut-off much harder. Be sure you are getting out of your opponent's way after return the serve. The Official Rules state you must give your opponent a down the line shot and a reasonable cross court angle.

Please refer to the following pictures.

This serve is obviously different than the others, so hit it well and get into position because your opponent will be ready for it in advance.

The angle for this serve is exactly the same as the other Drive Z to the backhand. The only difference is the serve is contact and travels much higher than the other. The object is still the same...get the ball into the left corner and force your opponent into a weak return. I am contacting the ball above my waist and hitting up on it to execute this serve.

Recovering to good court position

You should think of your serve motion as five steps, not just two. (see diagram on the following page) Hitting a good serve is critical, so concentrate on the motion and do it as well as you can. But, unless you hit an ace every time, you must prepare for the rally. Try to think of not just the two steps into the serve, but also the three steps back into good position. Push off your left foot and get back to good court position as soon as possible.

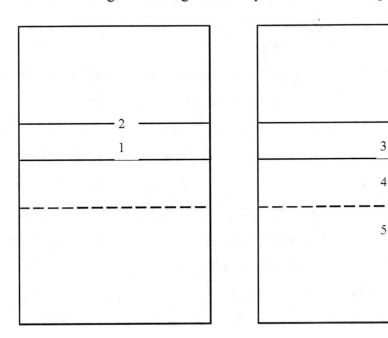

5 steps: **1. Right foot**   **3. Left foot**
                2. Left foot   **4. Right foot**
                                     5. Left foot

After stepping with the right and striding into your serve with the left foot, push off this same foot. This will help you get your feet set and get back into good court position as efficiently as possible.

The trade-off

After completing your service motion, you may have to settle for court position which is "good enough". Because of the fact that the drive serve gets to the receiver so quickly, you may not have time to get all the way behind the five foot line. This is the trade-off on the drive serve: you do not have time to get in perfect court position before the receiver hits the ball, but if you have executed a good serve, he or she should have a difficult first shot due to the pace and accuracy of the drive serve.

Because you may get stuck a little too far forward in the court, you are susceptible to a good down the line pass. Provided that you hit a good serve, your opponent should not be able to "tee off" and hit a great shot off of your serve. But, if you hit a less than perfect serve, be sure you defend the easiest shot for them to hit...the cross court. A splat will also come right to you and down the line should be the hardest shot for the receiver to hit. The main thing to keep in mind is that you must **get stopped**, regardless of whether you are in the ideal court position or not; and be prepared to move in any direction to cover the return of serve. If you are still in motion (backing up), then it will be difficult to cover a good splat because you are moving in the wrong direction. It will be difficult to stop your momentum and quickly change directions. It will also be difficult to plant and push off to cover the down the line shot should your opponent hit a good pass.

Patterns

Try to think of a specific pattern to use during a match. You should hit most of your serves straight to the backhand corner, but you must set that serve up by hitting a variety of other serves, too. Avoid being too predictable, like doing a two here, one there pattern. Strive to hit 50% of your serves to the backhand corner, 30% to the forehand (mix of Z's and straight in serves) and the remaining 20% as jam serves or wrap-around serves. A good sequence would go as follows:

1. Drive to the backhand
2. Drive to the backhand
3. Drive Z to the forehand
4. Jam to the backhand

5. Straight to the backhand
6. Wrap around to the forehand
7. Straight to the forehand
8. Straight to the backhand

You do not need to map out your entire service game and try to remember a 30 serve sequence. If you can remember these eight serves and where you are in the rotation, you will be in good shape. Establish the other serves to make your straight to the backhand serve better. Don't let someone camp on that serve.

Words to live by…

When you do find a serve that is working, be sure that you keep looking for two other serves you can also rely on. This applies to drive serves and lob serves, or a combination of both. You do not want to find yourself in a tie-breaker where your opponent has been looking at the same serve for two games and is starting to dial in on it. Now what? It's the tie-breaker and you no longer have a serve to rely on. Avoid this dilemma by finding a serve that works, and then finding two more that work, as well. I like to throw my other serves into the mix every once in a while just to remind my opponent that I have alternative plans which I can score with. It also helps to keep them from cheating over to cover the serve that I am using most often. Most people's weaknesses get worse over the course of a match, but some players do get used to a serve, or at least find a way to deal with the serve as the match progresses. Don't be one dimensional, it's dangerous.

"The only way to defeat a better player is to find three serves which give you a quality opportunity to score points. The third shot is the most important shot of the rally, and without good scoring opportunities, you are not likely to win."

Andy Roberts

Section Summary--Drive serves

--Decide in advance what serve you are going to hit.

--Find your starting position in the service box.

--Begin your motion with a small step, then drop the ball, and then a bigger step.   Shoulder turn and hip snap are critical.

--Watch the ball until the racquet contacts the ball.

--Recover into good court position as soon as possible. This may mean settling for "good enough" position. Be sure to get stopped.

--Turn and watch your opponent hit the ball.

--Keep track of what serves are working and which are not.

--The third shot of the rally is the most critical. Give yourself good scoring chances by hitting a variety of good serves.

--Don't be stubborn and force your favorite serve into play. Find the ones that your opponent dislikes, not just the ones you like.

知识就是力量

Knowledge is Power

Returning Serve

Starting position

When you walk back to receive serve, make sure you are in the proper starting position for the return. To check this, turn and face the back wall and reach out with your racquet and touch the wall. If the top of your racquet touches the wall without leaning into it, you're in business. (Remember to turn around and face the front wall again.) Be sure you do not get too far forward when returning serve, it will force you to step toward the back corner and disrupt your footwork. You are better off getting behind the ball and stepping parallel to the side wall for a forehand and at 45 degrees for a backhand.

Once you are in the correct starting position, assume a strong stance by bending at the knees and staying on the balls of your feet. Lean slightly forward and start with a backhand grip, since this is where most of the serves will be going. ***The goal is to take two steps to every serve.*** Be sure to begin your movement to the ball with the foot that is on the same side of the court as the ball. In other words, if the serve goes into the left corner, step with the left foot first, and then cross over with the right. This is the most efficient way to move around the racquetball court. The main benefit of this is that your feet are already set up to hit the return you want when you get there. As fast as racquetball is, you do not have time to get to the serve and then fix your feet, and you do not want to be hitting shots with bad footwork and open stances when return serve.

The return of serve is critical to your success in a match. If you cannot effectively neutralize a big serve or hit the proper shots off of a lob serve, then you will be hard pressed to win. The server has most of the advantages, but not necessarily all of them.

Good footwork and smart choices will help to reverse the server's advantage. One way of relieving some of the pressure during a match is not to give anything away, force your opponent to *earn* all of his points.

The following are Four rules for the
Return of Serve you <u>must</u> live by:

Rule #1

Never, ever skip a serve return. The worse thing you can do to yourself is to hand a free point to your opponent without making them hit anything but a serve to you. Strive to reduce your service return errors to an absolute minimum.

Rule #2

Don't take stupid shots. Sounds easy enough, doesn't it? You would probably be shocked at how many bad choices most people make on the return of serve. A low percentage shot is just that...low percentage! You cannot afford to take five or six tries at a certain shot until you finally hit one good shot. You have given away up to five points and gained only a side out for your efforts.

Rule #3

Hit a pass. It is as simple as that. If you hit a shot that is knee high or higher, you will force your opponent to leave center court to retrieve that shot. By hitting a pinch or a splat, you are going for broke. If you make the shot, you are OK; but you have very little room for error because the shot has to bounce twice in front of the service box to be effective. If you leave this shot up, you have given your opponent a front court set-up and you are very likely to lose most of those rallies.

The better choice is a good pass, which should be about knee high and bounce for the first time **behind** the serve box. Aiming this high greatly reduces the chance of skipping the ball and giving away a free point. If you leave this shot up, at least you are forcing your opponent to chase down your shot and you will have time to get into good court position. This is playing the percentages. Only after getting your opponent used to the fact that you are hitting the ball deep into the court should you begin to occasionally mix in some splats.

Exception: If your opponent hits a drive serve that comes well off the back wall, many times the server will hurry back into center court. This gives you more room to hit a pinch or splat in front of them. Often, you will catch them in that in-between spot while still moving backwards to center court and it is difficult to switch directions quickly enough to cover a good splat.

Rule #4

A good ceiling ball game is highly underrated. If you are not presented with a reasonable opportunity off of the serve, go to the ceiling. This will pull your opponent out of center court and allow you time to take good court position. Obviously, you cannot expect to hit a poor ceiling ball and win the majority of the rallies. This shot must be practiced as much as the other shots, if not more. *A good ceiling game is the foundation of solid racquetball.* Make your opponent take shots from 38 feet as often as possible, and things will likely go your way.

Attacking the lob serve

If you have the opportunity to cut off a lob serve and hit an intelligent return, by all means do so. Do not, however, fall into the trap your opponent is setting for you. They want you to attempt to kill the ball out of the air, which is probably the toughest shot in racquetball to execute. Be sure you mix your shots, with most of them going down the line. Since most people play too far forward, a pass is an effective choice against players who fall into this category. If they are hitting serves which do not give you the option of going down the line, be intelligent with your return of serve. If you do choose to cut the ball off, here are some things to keep in mind:

1   **Get your feet set early**.

This means seeing the ball hit the front wall and being in   position to hit the serve before it gets past the service box. Remember that your last step into the ball should be at a 45 degree angle, so be sure to move straight forward and then over to the ball.

2   **Avoid trying to kill the ball in front of your opponent.**

It is entirely too difficult to consistently take the ball out of the air and make it bounce twice before your opponent can get to it. Save that for when you break into the Top Ten on Tour.

3. Perfect Practice makes perfect.

Be sure that you are very confident with cutting the serve off.

Develop this confidence in practice, <u>before</u> trying it in a match.

4. Move like a Knight. (the chess piece)

Be sure you move straight forward and then over to the ball instead of going straight towards the ball. This will give you a better angle of approach and help minimize your errors. Two steps forward, and one over, into the shot. This will help you avoid being too close to the ball and being forced into a cross court shot.

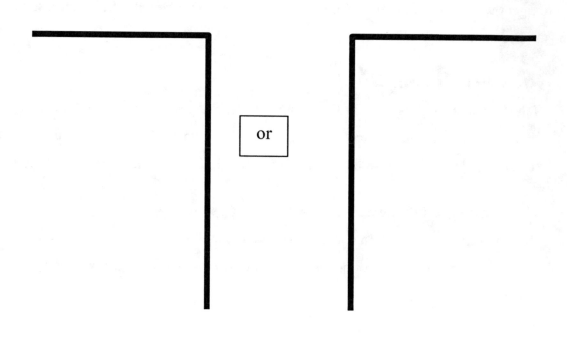

Watching the ball

I cannot stress enough how important it is to watch the ball. The two most important things in racquetball are seeing the ball and footwork to the shots.

Whether it is on the return of serve or during the rally, your eyes must stay on the ball as long as possible, into the hitting zone where you will make contact. In general, use a wide view of the court with a soft focus. This will allow you to see the ball and your opponent at the same time. As the ball gets closer to you, narrow your vision to just the ball and then just the label on the ball. You should strive to see the ball disappear from the spot your racquet made contact with it. This skill can be enhanced with practice. Think of your target, see the ball and swing! You may want to check into a Sports Vision Therapy Program to enhance your ability to see the ball. It made a huge difference in my career. I can see the label on a new ball during the rally after graduating from a Sports Vision Therapy Program.

If you can't do this, at least try to develop the ability to see the ball clearly in your hitting zone. The ball may be blurry during flight, but when it gets to your hitting zone you switch from peripheral to central focus. You will be much more consistent in hitting the sweet spot and therefore, more consistent with your shots.

You must turn and watch the ball at all times during the rallies. This means watching the ball as it goes into the back corner with your opponent chasing it down. By turning and watching what happens behind you, you are far less likely to get hit by your

opponent's shot. You'll know when it's going to be close and you can give them more room to swing. You also are increasing your time of seeing the ball to <u>twice</u> what it would be if you just looked at the front wall. This will greatly increase your chance of covering the next shot. Plus, as discussed several places in this book, your opponent may give you clues as to where they are hitting their next shot. By opening their stance or closing their stance, they are giving you clues you would not see if you did not turn and follow the ball. **This practice should be done only when you are wearing protective eye-wear.**

知识就是力量

Knowledge is Power

Section Summary—the Return of Serve

--Be sure your starting position is centered in the court, an arm and racquets length away from the back wall.

--Make sure you are on the balls of your feet, weight slightly forward, with a backhand grip.

--Follow the Four Rules of Serve Return: Never skip a return. Don't take stupid shots. Hit a pass when you can. Use a ceiling ball when in doubt.

--Be sure to practice attacking lob serve before being that aggressive in a match.

--Practice watching the ball and switching from a soft focus (peripheral) to a hard focus (central focus). Learn the appropriate times to use each one.

I must give credit where it is due. The following section concerning court coverage was taught to me by Andy Roberts. I wanted to thank him for his contribution to my game.

Here it is… The essence of Percentage Racquetball. Thank you for your patience, but hopefully you found the previous information helpful.

Court Coverage

Racquetball is constantly changing from offense to defense and back again. You must appreciate that opportunities are created in properly trained split second decisions and good footwork. It is difficult, but not impossible, to hit good shots without your feet set underneath you. Trust me when I say that you are much better off doing it the easy way and getting your feet set to hit most of your shots. There will be plenty of times when that is not possible anyway, so don't increase the frequency of those times when you don't get set. **Footwork is the fine line between offensive chances and true set -ups.**

One of the main reasons this system is so effective against nearly everyone you will face is the fact that most people give very little thought to percentages and appropriate shots. Most players have poor footwork and therefore are forced to hit the shot the ball presents to them, versus having options. The people who do actually think about strategy are just basically trying to hit the ball away from their opponent. The problem with this theory is that you are always hitting the ball in the direction your opponent is running to get back into center court. The exchange ends up being a bunch of cross court shots. While this will work in some cases, most of the time you would be better off hitting the ball back to where your opponent hit their last shot from. They should no longer be standing there, because they should be hustling back into center court position. If you happen to be playing someone who is lazy, or who swings and evaluates their shot from that position, this is the time to employ the cross court theory. If you are playing someone like this, your match should be a piece of cake.

***If you have ever watched good tennis players play, a lot of rallies force the opponent to run to the corner, back to the middle and then back to the same corner they just came from.

It is much more difficult and tiring to overcome your body's inertia to switch directions than it is to run in a straight line to cover a shot. You should apply this same strategy to your game.

Old school court position
(otherwise known as the hard way)

Most of the books ever written about racquetball talk about a "floating court position." This is a standard way of thinking in racquetball, however, that does not mean it is the best way. This system has some major flaws to it; please refer to the following explanation:

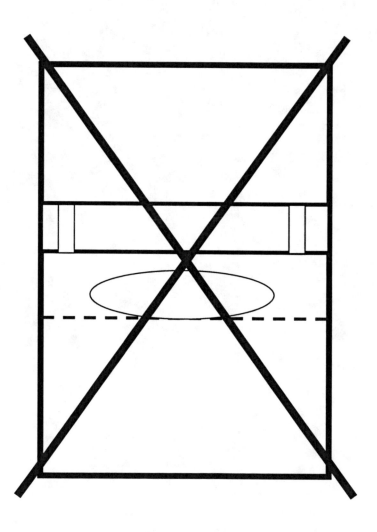

1. This system covers the killshot. Both the down the line pass and a cross court pass get by them.

2. You must read the shot that is coming and adjust your position accordingly. If you play new players,   it is tough to read where they are hitting their next shot.

3. You will need very fast hands to play that close to the front wall. Left up shots and passes are landing right at your feet and become tough shots to defend.

4. Luckily for you, most people still play this way, and Percentage Racquetball exploits these weaknesses every rally.

Defensive position

How much of the court do you really cover?

Bear in mind you are not covering all 800 square feet of a racquetball court. **Percentage Racquetball** means you will cover the easy shots and make your opponent beat you if they can by making the tough shots. This can be looked on as "Vegas odds". Your opponent is going to make *some* of the shots you give them but they will not likely make the *majority* of them. Las Vegas is built on the principal of "you win some of the time, but we win most of the time." Did you notice they are always adding new hotels and casinos in that town?

Remember also that you are not going to run closer to any of the walls than an arm and racquet length away. Only when the ball is touching the side wall should you be as close as a racquet and arm's length. Since most shots are not "wallpaper", the area you cover is smaller than you think. This reduces the area of the court by quite a bit, especially in the back court. If your feet enter this zone, you are over-running the ball and you will have to change your swing to accommodate this footwork error.

Please see the following diagram.

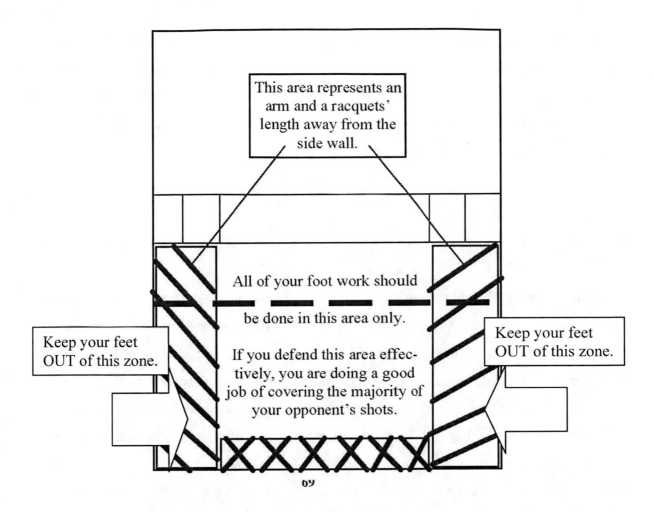

This area represents an arm and a racquets' length away from the side wall.

All of your foot work should be done in this area only.

If you defend this area effectively, you are doing a good job of covering the majority of your opponent's shots.

Keep your feet OUT of this zone.

Keep your feet OUT of this zone.

A hard hit kill shot will rebound and carry deeper into the court than most people realize. The second bounce will be around the short line of the service box, so there is <u>no reason</u> to be in front of the five foot line. It is always easier to move forward into the court to cover a kill than it is to move backward to cover a pass. **This is the most common flaw in the majority of people's thinking about court coverage.** Most players want to cover kill shots when in reality their opponents hit many more passes than kills. If you are

EKTELON
PLAY WITH FIRE

cheating forward in the court (in front of the five foot line), you are making your opponent's job easier by allowing them to hit passes around you. This means they can hit a shot which is three feet high to win, instead of a two inch high kill shot: which do you think is easier to execute? Besides, you would be surprised how infrequently a true kill shot is hit. I would be willing to bet it is far less often than you think.

Rule #1

There is no reason to be in front of the five foot line for your defensive court coverage.

By standing one step out of the middle of the court, on the opposite side of the court from your opponent, you will cover more shots effectively. Here is why: From the left corner of the court, a cross court shot and a splat will both end up on the right side of the court. Only a down the line shot ends up on the left side of the court. This means simply by standing still in this position, you will be covering two of the three offensive opportunities your opponent will have. Obviously if they roll out their shot, you cannot cover it, but you cannot really cover that shot no matter where you are standing. The idea is that you will cover *most* of the shots, and you will cover most of the shots in two steps (covered in the footwork section). This court position will give you more time to set up, give you better chances to execute you shot, and puts pressure on your opponent to kill the ball or hit a perfect pass to win the rally. If they go down the line, you are in reasonable position to cover that shot, too. This is the most difficult shot to win the rally with, because your opponent's margin for error is very small. The down the line pass has to bounce twice before the back wall, not hit the side wall, and not get pulled down the middle to get past you. Since you are playing a little deeper in the court, you have more time to cover the down the line shot.

Rule #2

Always cover the cross court shot. This is the easiest shot to hit in racquetball, so take it away from your opponent.

From your opponent's perspective, it looks like you are giving them two-thirds of the court to hit their next shot into. The fact of the matter is, you are covering the easiest shot to hit, the cross court, and are in good position to cover any splat which has not bounced twice in front of the service box. They will quickly realize that they cannot hit the ball around you very often, because your new, deeper court position puts you in a better position to defend those shots. They will have to hit kills and perfect passes to beat you.

In this scenario, my opponent has hit a low cross court pass; I have moved forward and am hitting my shot down the line.

This is where you want to cover the court from. By taking away the cross court, effectively covering the splat, and defending most of the down the line shots, you will put the maximum amount of pressure on your opponent. They will now need to hit nearly perfect shots to win rallies against you.

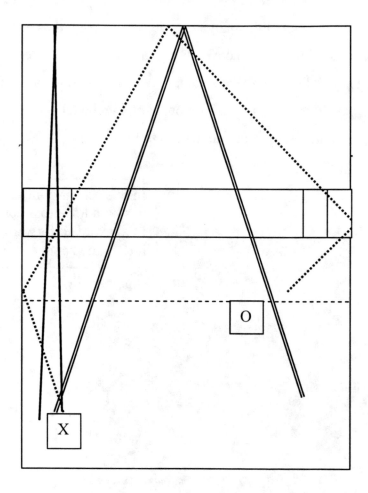

This diagram illustrates the proper court position when your opponent is in the deep left corner. As you can see from the path of each shot, two of the three shots come right to you.

Theory in action

Percentage Racquetball never fails.

After serving a lob serve, assume good court position in a spot one step out of the middle, away from the side to which you served. In other words, after you serve a lob to the left corner, assume your court position one step to the right of center. You want to be behind the five foot line; with the right foot touching the line and the left foot slightly deeper than the front, shoulder width apart. You should stand with knees bent and your weight on the balls of your feet. You will want to have a forehand grip when you have served to the left side. This is because the percentages are weighted very heavily that you will end up hitting a forehand. Your opponent is more likely to hit a cross court or a splat, both of which end up being a forehand for you. This is important because some of the shots you defend are going to be tough shots, ones that land right at your feet or shots that send you scrambling to the front court. Be sure to have your racquet out in front of you and not pointing down towards the floor. This position should very closely simulate your return of serve position.

To reiterate, you are putting pressure on your opponent simply by standing in this position on the court. You can effectively defend the cross court and the splat, as well as cover most of the down the line shots. You will force them to kill the ball in front of you, or hit nearly perfect passes to win rallies. Obviously, you are going to make errors even from this position. You are not perfect. But by playing the percentages, this means that *most* of the time things should work out in your favor. If you adopt this court coverage and choose the right shot in reply to your opponent's, you will win the majority of the time. The beauty of

this system is that if you are not sure where your opponent is hitting the ball, you hold still and be correct most of the time. Don't guess and get caught out of position.

Train yourself to not move from that position until you are sure where the ball is going to end up. This is critical to your success.

知识就是力量

Knowledge is Power

Section Summary---Court Coverage

-- Always cover the cross court shot. Play the percentages by staying

on the opposite side of the court from your opponent.

-- Do not guess. You are better off not moving until you are sure where the ball is

going versus guessing and being beaten by a bad shot just because you are

out of position.

-- Strive to cover every offensive shot in two steps. This does not include

shots that are playable off the back wall.

-- Your footwork patterns are very set once you get the hang of them, so be sure

you get into the correct position every time. (This will be covered in the

following chapter)

-- Be sure your racquet is up and ready all the time. Do not get caught with

your racquet at your feet and have no choice but to push the ball.

Percentage Racquetball never fails; do not stray from it.

> **"A golden rule is to never use a more complex move than necessary to achieve a desired result."**
>
> **Bruce Lee**

Footwork

Efficiency is critical to your success. If you can minimize your movement, and yet still cover the court effectively, you are saving energy and putting pressure on your opponent at the same time. You must learn to lead with the foot which is on the same side of the court where the ball is going to end up. In other words, if I hit a backhand splat, the ball will travel to the right side of the court. This means you will step with your right foot and then cross over with your left. This is the epitome of efficiency...you will have your feet set upon arrival to the ball, and have options as to where you can hit the next shot. ***Bad footwork equals limited choices***. With bad footwork you will probably be forced into a cross court kill or worse a reverse pinch. Yikes!!! These are two shots which must be hit perfectly to work. By using the proper footwork to the shots, you will give yourself choices each time, instead of the ball choosing the shot for you.

You must learn the footwork appropriate to each shot hit by your opponent. Strive to cover almost every offensive shot in two steps--no more and no less. The first step is the adjustment step. This means that if the ball is close to the middle, a small step and a cross over step will suffice. If the ball is close to the side wall, a big first step and a big cross over step will be necessary to cover the shot. Ideally you would always split the distance to the ball equally between the two steps to the ball. **Understand that you always want to adjust with your feet and not your swing.** If your feet get you into position properly, you never

have to change your stroke. This of course is not possible to do every time, but the more often you accomplish this, the better you will be.

For some strange reason, everyone wants to cross over first and then step with the other foot. Apparently, it is not human nature to step first and then cross over to move to a shot. The latter, however, is much more efficient. Efficiency is crucial to success. You must retrain yourself to move in this manner; it will help you have options on every shot because your feet will be set correctly each time. You will use less energy, you will get into good court position sooner and consequently force your opponent to kill the ball in front of you, or hit perfect passes to win. This will take much practice, on and off the court, with and without the ball. When you master this principle, it will be as though your legs see the ball and react accordingly.

Good court position and efficient footwork will do several things for you:

1. You are set to defend the easiest and most common return of serve, the cross court. The easiest shot to hit is cross court; all your opponent has to do is hit the front wall somewhere in the middle. Never give your opponent the easy way out.

2. You are in good position to defend a splat or pinch. Any left up splat will come right to you. A poorly-executed pinch will do the same.

3. You can cover <u>most</u> of the down the line shots that are hit. Your opponent will have to hit very good passes to win rallies from deep court. You will <u>at least</u> be able to hit a

ceiling ball off even a good pass from this court position. Your footwork will get you to their shot in time and you will be set to hit the shot when you arrive at the ball.

4. You are forcing your opponent to consistently hit difficult shots to beat you. Killing the ball in front of someone who is in good court position is very difficult, especially from the deep court. Hitting passes that a person in good court position cannot cover is almost as difficult as a kill from the deep court.

Percentage Racquetball never fails.

The Third Shot

The most important shot in racquetball is the third shot of every rally. If you are serving well and getting weak returns from your opponent, your job of scoring points and winning becomes much easier. If you are hitting bad returns and taking high risk shots, your opponent is winning that battle.

The person who dictates the third shot of the rally a majority of the time most likely will be winning the match. You must consider this; it is the true measure of your serve and your opponent's return, and your opponents' serve and your return. If you are losing this battle, you must re-evaluate your serving strategy. If you are not getting a good third shot, or are giving your opponent an easy third shot, you are going to lose if that trend continues. Find an alternative way to win, or call time-out and ask the tournament director if there is a consolation bracket.

Bear in mind, you are evaluating the quality of your opportunity, not the result. If you are skipping an easy set-up from mid court, that is your fault and not a function of your opponent's return. If you are not capitalizing on this chance, you had better start. If you are skipping balls, try aiming higher and hitting passes instead of kills or pinches. You need to score when you get the opportunity, so figure something out that will work. Just because your opponent is cutting off the serve doesn't mean that they are winning that exchange. It may not be the most comfortable thing in the world, but if you are getting quality chances you are winning the battle on paper. If you are skipping balls or not winning rallies, that is your fault. Don't change a winning game plan.

Getting your opponent to play into *your* strengths.

You should choose serves that will give you a shot with which you are comfortable. If you are not very good at hitting balls from deep court, then hitting a nick lob serve to the backhand is probably not a great idea. Think about what shot your opponent is likely to hit off of the serve you are about to choose, and if that suits you, great! If not, then hit a serve that is going to give you a reply you can deal with. Personally, I love re-killing the ball in the front court *and* taking the ball off the back wall, so either option my opponent takes is fine with me. If you are not adept at one of these, either get better at it or try not to give your opponent that option. (Get better at it!)

A good drive serve will get you into a bang-bang rhythm, giving you quick shots and forcing you into split-second decisions. If this "serve and shoot" style is more suited to how you would like to play, then by all means, force the pace of the game. A lob serve will get you into a slower, more methodical game style. If that suits you better, or at least is uncomfortable for your opponent, stick to it and win. It is good to be able to do both, even if you much prefer one over the other.

> **"The primary thing to consider when you draw your sword**
> **is that your intention is to cut your enemy, whatever the means.**
> **There is a huge difference between cutting and slashing.**
> **When you cut, your spirit is resolved."**
> **Miyamoto Musashi**

Shot selection

I believe it is very important to <u>commit</u> to a shot and hit it with <u>conviction</u>. Trust your swing and don't alter it halfway through. If you realize you have mis-timed a shot, go with it. You are better off mistakenly hitting the ball cross court with a solid swing and *intent* than you are trying to slice the ball down the line when your opponent is set up in front of you. You can still win with a solid cross court, even if your opponent is standing in reasonable court position. You will be hard pressed to slice a ball down the line and get it by your opponent. It is likely the shot will kick off the side wall and come out to the middle of the court. Then you are in trouble. You usually will be better off continuing the swing and hitting your intended down the line shot cross court. If you have hit the ball at the correct height (knee high), even if you pull the shot down the middle, it will be difficult for your opponent to handle. This shot will hit right at your opponent's feet, and be very difficult to do much with.

Now, when you're in the front court, I believe the opposite is true. If you over-run the ball, swing too soon, whatever, and you know a down the line shot will win the rally, do whatever is necessary to get the ball down the line. Slice, chop, do everything short of breaking your wrist to get the ball where it needs to go. You are in position to win the rally, so do it! Sometimes even with the best footwork, things don't work out the way you expected, so learn to make do. This is the time to deviate from what I said in the last paragraph, because your opponent is probably out of position. You have worked to gain the upper hand in this rally, so take advantage and make the shot. You do not need to smash every shot or flat roll it to win.

The True Definition of Shot Selection

Ultimately, the correct shot is dictated by your opponent's court position. You must be aware of where the other player is standing when you are hitting your shots. The right shot is not based on whether or not you roll out your shot, but rather, if you leave the ball up, are you still in the rally? If you hit lots of pinches, you are likely to pay the price for most of the shots you leave up. It is tough to win this way all of the time. That is the essence of this book--leaving yourself margin for error and putting yourself in position to win most of the time.

The following section will cover the shots and how, why, and when to use them. **Bear in mind, the correct shot is dictated by your opponents court position.** The "textbook" shot may differ from the appropriate shot because people play the game differently. You must learn to see the whole court. What I am about to propose is a difficult but important skill. **You must learn to feel what your opponent is doing in the rallies.** By this, I mean learning to hear when someone gets planted in center court or when they are still scrambling. Your opponent cannot move forward quickly if his feet are planted parallel to the front wall. To move forward, one foot must be moved back to push off. If your opponent is still scrambling around in the back court, say after a dive, you do not want to hit a pass. Use your peripheral vision to assess your opponent's position in the court and take advantage of their mistakes. These are invaluable skills when playing racquetball, especially if you are playing an opponent with whom you are unfamiliar. You must start noticing these things; it will make your job on the court much easier.

The beauty of this system is that it nearly eliminates the need for strategy beyond following the system itself. Percentage Racquetball emphasizes percentages, most of the time things will happen in your favor. Be sure to do your job within the System, and you will have a fundamentally sound game plan against any player you face.

The Shots

Down the Line

The best shot in the game. This should become the basis of your game. The passing shot is critical to success in racquetball. You must utilize the whole court and make your opponent run to the corners. The court is twice as long as it is wide, therefore, it is logical that you should hit twice as many passes as pinches. **A good pass will bounce between the short line and the five foot line on the first bounce and carry deep into the back court.** A "left-up" kill shot is not a good pass. If your opponent is in center court position, it is easily retrieved by your opponent. This is because the ball will lose half of its speed when it hits the floor. Use this to your advantage by making the ball land even with where your opponent is standing.

Most people play too far forward in the court. Hitting a pass is the perfect shot against this type of player. If you choose to hit a pinch or a splat, the player who is standing too far up front is in good position to cover the shot. It has to be nearly perfect to work, and trust me, you don't want to <u>have</u> to be nearly perfect very often. If you leave this shot up in the front court, you are probably going to lose that rally. A pass, on the other hand, will travel deep into the court and will win the rally if hit properly. If you should hit the ball too high and it comes off the back wall, your opponent still has to run to the back court to hit their next shot. (The more running you make your opponent do, the higher the chance for an error.) This gives you the opportunity to move into good court position to defend the next shot. This is **Percentage Racquetball**, the essence of the system. Always leave yourself an "out", a safety valve. This means if you miss the shot, you are still going to have a reasonable chance to win the rally.

Please see the diagram on the next page.

However, if you play an opponent who is hugging the line, or obviously moving that direction every time you hit the ball, you will need to change your strategy accordingly. It may be the "textbook" shot to go down the line, but if your opponent is standing there or leaning that direction, you are playing into their game plan. Learn to see your opponent's court position and choose your shots accordingly. Use your peripheral vision to focus on the ball and still see your opponent at the same time. Narrow your vision to just the ball as it gets to you. Bear in mind, a player who covers the line is making your job easier by leaving the cross court shot open. If you hit your opponent in an attempt to go cross court, that is an avoidable hinder. The official rules state the player hitting the shot is entitled to a down the line and a reasonable cross court angle (from one corner of the back court to the opposite corner of the back court). This means you can have the cross court but not a reverse pinch.

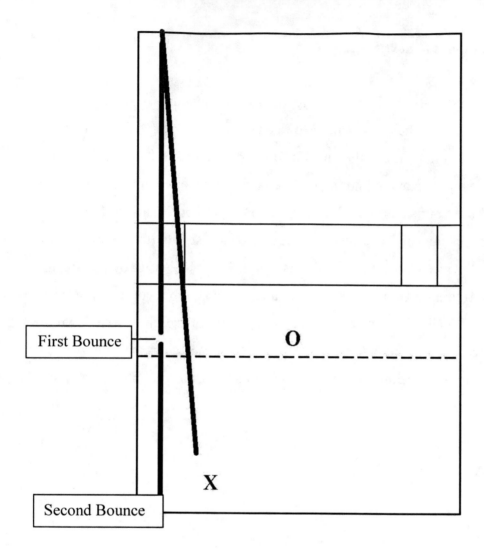

First Bounce

O

Second Bounce

X

O is your opponent in typical front court position. You can see why a passing shot works against a player who plays this far forward. X is the player hitting the down the line shot from deep court.

Cross Court

Since most players play too far forward in the court, a good cross court pass is also very effective and typically easier to execute than a down the line pass. The definition of a good cross court pass is a shot which is hit about knee high or higher and lands behind the service box on the first bounce. The shot should hit the floor twice before the back wall or at least strike the back wall very low. A wide-angle pass hits the side wall behind the five foot line on the fly and hits low enough that it does not come off the back wall or at least low enough not to be playable. This is tougher to defend than a regular cross court pass but is also more difficult to execute. Luckily, a regular cross court pass should usually be good enough to win the rally.

When a person is playing too far forward, they are susceptible to both the cross court and the down the line pass. A match against such an opponent should be the easiest to win. You can hit <u>knee high</u> shots all day and win most of the rallies...piece of cake.

Most of the people who play racquetball play too far forward.

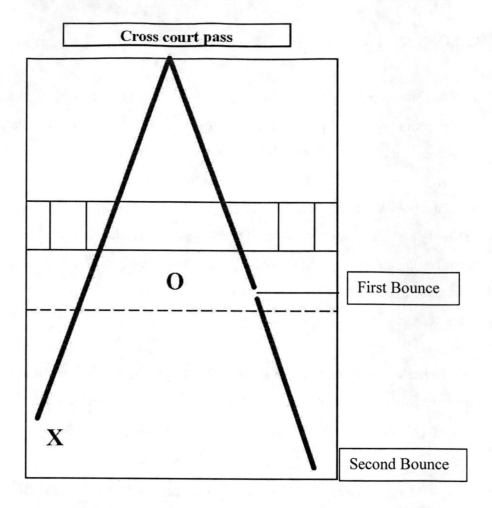

Cross court pass

O

X

First Bounce

Second Bounce

This is the most common shot in racquetball. If hit at the correct height, it is very effective. Most players hit this shot too low, which allows someone who is playing too far forward a good chance to re-kill this shot.

Note where the first bounce should be.

Pinch

A pinch is a shot that hits the front right or left corner, impacting the side wall first, and then the front wall. It should be hit about six inches high, and bounce twice before the service box. It is a good shot in the right situation. Whenever your opponent is behind you is a good time for a pinch. Avoid hitting pinches when your opponent is in front of you, because, if you miss, you're in trouble. This shot takes some proficiency; because unlike the pass, a left-up pinch is a set up in center court for your opponent.

If your opponent does give you a front court set-up, be sure to put the ball away. Take a little pace off your shot and be sure to hit it well. You are only 10 to 20 feet away from the front wall, so you should be able to execute this shot with high frequency. Practice this until it is a foregone conclusion, for both you and your opponent, that this set-up is going to be put away.

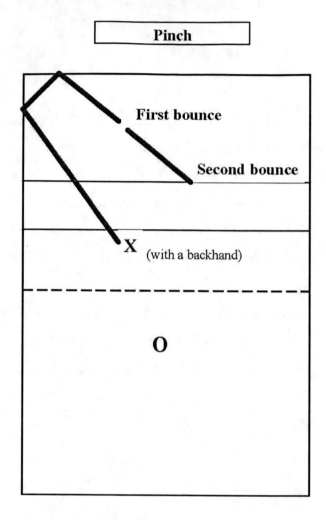

The pinch is a shot which should be executed when your opponent is behind you. When you force a weak return, or your opponent tries to execute a pinch from the deep court and does not make it bounce twice before you can retrieve it, this is the time to implement this shot.

If you choose to hit a pass in this situation, it will need to be perfect to work, because your opponent is already deep in the court.

Reverse Pinch

A **reverse pinch** is a variation of the pinch, it will be hit at an extreme cross court angle and strikes the side wall on the opposite side of the court first and then the front wall. There are two fundamental problems with a reverse pinch:

1. The ball is coming right back to the spot from which it was hit, so you may be creating a hinder if you don't execute it extremely well.

2. If you leave this shot up, you are out of position in the front court and your opponent can win with an easy cross court pass.

You should use this shot very sparingly if at all. It is difficult to execute, has no room for error, and is easily defended by your opponent if it is not hit perfectly.

Please see the next diagram.

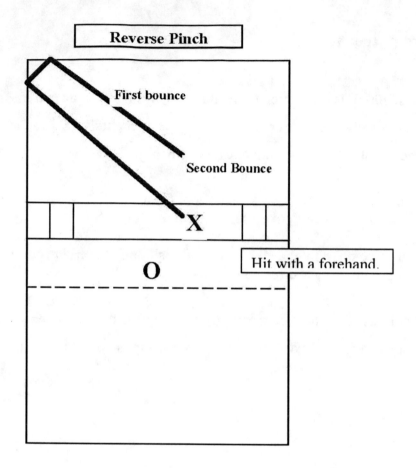

There are some problems with this shot, especially the fact that it has to be really good to work. If you do not execute it properly, the penalty is high for missing.

Splats

A splat is a shot which is hit from deep court directly into the side wall about three to five feet in front of your position in the deep court. It should hit the front wall in about the middle of the wall, bounce once before the side wall, hit the side wall and bounce quickly thereafter. To execute this shot, use the same set-up in terms of mechanics...racquet up high, good shoulder turn...and all the rest. The only change you want is to contact the ball deeper in your stance than a down the line shot. The splat should be hit deep in your stance, almost in line with your back foot. A good splat needs to be hit firmly; otherwise the desired effect does not take place. A firmly hit splat makes the ball change shape a little, and this is what creates the better angle. A softly hit splat will be "geometrically correct" and end up being just a wide pinch, which is less effective.

A good splat is an effective shot in the right situation. If you are playing someone who is playing too deep in the court, this is a good time for a splat. It is also a good shot to mix in *after* hitting a few down the line passes. After establishing the pass, your opponent is likely to be leaning towards the down the line shot and this gives you more room to hit the splat. It is also a good shot to hit against an opponent who is slow moving forward in the court. Most players move more effectively either front to back or side to side, few do both equally well.

Remember, the same rule applies to the splat as the pinch: if you leave this shot up in center court, your opponent has an easy next shot. Practice this shot and become proficient before using it regularly in a tournament. Bad splats are an opponent's dream. Use this shot sparingly; if you miss it, you are likely to lose that rally. If you miss a pass a little high, you are still forcing your opponent to move and hit another shot.

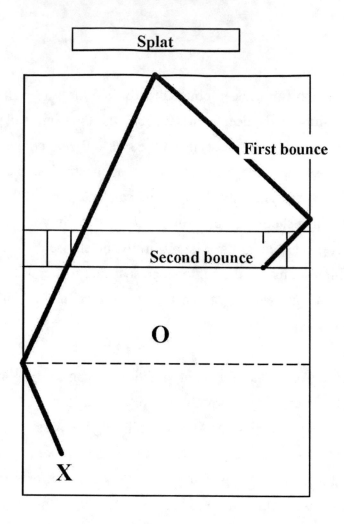

Bear in mind, you cannot hit the same shot over and over and expect it to work every time. Your opponent will begin to adapt to what you are doing if you do not change it up once in a while. You must mix in a few cross courts and an occasional splat to keep the down the line shot open. Use this to your advantage by keeping your opponent guessing.

Ceiling balls

The foundation of good racquetball.

Unlike most of the players who play tournament racquetball, I still believe in a good ceiling ball game. The common trend is to do what the pros do--shoot everything. Well, if you were good enough to make shots like the pro's, you would not have needed to buy this book, would you? That is the problem with watching the Pro and Open players. They do things that most players in racquetball cannot do with any consistency. But remember, they didn't hit those shots from the beginning; they built a good foundation of solid strokes and shots and then began to explore shots outside the normal ranges.

Executing a forehand ceiling ball is very similar to throwing a baseball. The same rules apply to the hitting zone...if you contact the ball even with your front foot, it will go cross court. If you hit the ball in the middle of your stance, it will go straight in. Start your swing from a "throwing" position, swing in an upward direction and swing smoothly to hit the ball at the desired contact point. Watch the ball until it hits the strings. Use a short follow-through to finish the shot.

***The foot position and grip are always the same for every forehand, regardless of the height of the ball. Be sure to get squared up to the side wall and do not slice the ball or draw the ball on the strings to hit a ceiling ball. This is too precise a move and will break down under pressure or fatigue.

To hit a backhand ceiling ball, start with your racquet about shoulder high, extended to the point just short of locking the elbow. Remember the rules of the hitting zone: a ball contacted even with the front foot will go straight in and a ball contacted in front of the front foot will go cross court. Watch the ball until the point of contact and be sure to follow through in an upward motion. The racquet should finish higher than its starting position. Strive to hit the ball flush and avoid slicing or drawing the racquet across the ball to hit this shot.

***The foot position should be the same for a backhand ceiling ball as it is for any other backhand--45 degree angle toward the side wall, feet shoulder width apart. The grip is also always the same. Be sure your eyes follow the ball into the racquet strings.

You should aim at the first set of lights away from the front wall (most courts were built with the lights about 10 feet from the front wall). By aiming here, you will create an angle suitable for hitting a good ceiling ball. The speed is the critical part of the equation. You must get a feel for the speed with which you need to hit this shot. Most players hit their ceiling balls too hard. It is much more difficult for your opponent to hit a ceiling ball that falls short of the back wall than one that is struck too hard and comes off the back wall.

Controlling a ceiling ball on the move is difficult, but VERY necessary. You must learn to control the shot even if you are diving. If you hit a poor ceiling ball, you should not expect to win that rally. If you do, you got lucky or your opponent did something wrong.

***When you play at higher elevations, aim farther back on the ceiling to help combat the effects of high altitude. You may still need to adjust the pace of the shot, too. If you are playing a tournament in a high altitude town, be sure to get there early to get dialed in.

Something to consider...

Try hitting your opponent some ceiling balls that are not right at the corner, but about eight feet away from the side wall. The reason for this is the angle is much tougher than hitting the shot straight in. If you assume good court position, the cross court is covered, a less than perfect splat will come right to you and your opponent has to hit a perfect shot to get the ball by you. Frequently, a down the line pass will kick off the side wall because of the angle needed to hit that shot into the left corner in deep court is beyond the control of most players.

Sometimes the shot will be pulled too much to the middle and will easily be reached from your good court position. Always make your opponent hit tough shots to win.

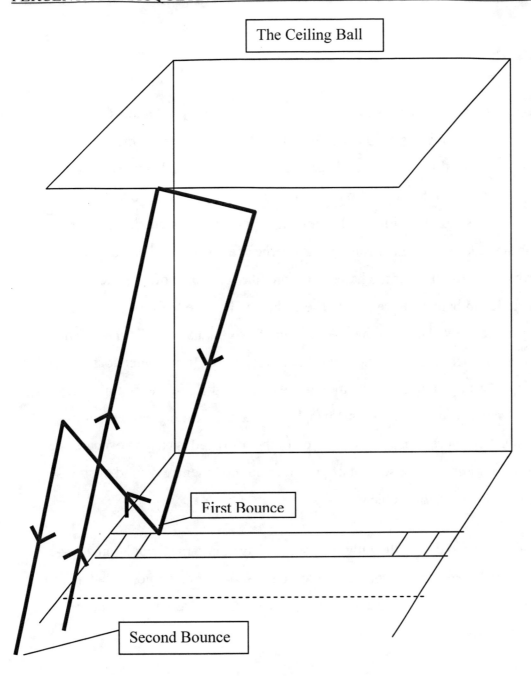

The Ceiling Ball

First Bounce

Second Bounce

Overheads

An overhead shot is a good idea in the right situation. When cutting off a lob serve, say a lob Z to the forehand, an overhead is a good shot to hit. Never, ever try to hit a kill or a splat from this position. Hitting a pass is easier to execute, and if you leave the shot up or hit it too hard, you're still in the rally. Your opponent will have to chase down the shot while you get into good court position and await your opportunity. A good overhead return for a lob serve to the forehand is to hit the overhead at 50% speed and about chest high on the front wall. If you hit it too hard, it is more likely to come off the back wall. The shot is designed to bounce in front of the serve box and be too high for your opponent to hit effectively. They will have to do one of two things...run the shot down in the back court or get sucked into taking a bad shot as they move from center court. Your opponent hitting a ceiling ball in this situation is not an immediate threat, so this is not a concern. By the way, it is difficult for most people to hit a good ceiling ball in this situation anyway. This more conservative version of the overhead is easy to execute, has lots of room for error and will cause a lot of grief for your opponent. My kind of shot--I love to make my opponents miserable.

When hitting an overhead during the rally, you should have the same thought process--ease of execution and high percentage. Don't try to roll out a shot from over your head, it's too hard to do. It is self-defeating to take a low percentage shot, and even worse to miss it. Stick to hitting <u>passes</u> on overheads.

When hitting an overhead shot, remember to take a little pace off and place it well. If you hit the ball about 8-10 feet high on the front wall, it should bounce around the service box and therefore force your opponent to short hop their next shot, or make them chase the ball to the deep court.

You can also hit a wide angle pass, aiming for the left side wall on the fly, about even with the five foot line. If you do this shot correctly, it will be a tough shot for your opponent to handle.

Section Summary -- Shot Selection

-- Establish your down the line shot early.

-- Choose your shots wisely. Always ask yourself if I do not execute the shot perfectly, am I still going to be in the rally?

-- Passes should become the basis of your game. Do not play into your opponents position and hit shots into the front corners.

-- Hit splats and pinches sparingly, only when you have your opponent out of position.

-- Be aware of what your opponent is doing during the rally. This is ultimately what dictates your shot selection.

-- Ceiling balls are still very effective, especially against today's aggressive players. It will force your opponent into the deep court and allow you to set up your court position and capitalize on the errors and opportunities your opponent gives you.

-- Overheads are a good idea when hit appropriately. Do not try to hit kills from this position. Stick to hitting passes and wait for a true opportunity to win the rally.

--Because the game has evolved into power and hitting kill shots, a de-emphasis has been placed on hitting passes. Because of this, a lot of good players are in a position to be defeated when they are not executing perfectly. Their game style will create opportunities for everyone who learns this system.

> "To become a Champion requires a conditioning of readiness
> that causes the individual to approach with pleasure
> even the most tedious practice sessions."
> --Bruce Lee

Drills

Practice drills

Things to consider about your practice sessions.

First and foremost, practice sessions are when you get better. Don't muddle your way through them if you're sick, tired, bored, injured or just not in the right frame of mind. You are trying to replace what you previously did with what you want to be doing. Don't be sloppy, careless, or lazy when practicing, because it will show in your match play. You are teaching your body discipline, so when you play matches you can turn your brain off and turn your disciplined body loose.

Never mistake activity for achievement.

Second, quality is much better than quantity. You are way better off having a 45 minute intense and focused practice than to spend two hours smacking the ball around with poor focus and little intent. You will not get better just by standing on the hardwood.

Third, you should base your practice time and frequency on what *you* need. If you are an A player, you may already have a solid forehand from most places in the court. That's fine, do those drills sparingly and focus mostly on backhands. If you are a C level player, you should do all the drills as often as you can in order to improve your level of play. You must be very honest with yourself when assessing strengths and weaknesses. You may want to ask some of your friends for advice or videotape a match and analyze the footage. Be prepared though, you may not be as pretty as you think you are. No one ever is.

The harder you work, the harder it is to make you surrender.

OK, time to go to work. It is time to roll up your sleeves, punch the clock and improve your ability on the court. There is no substitute for a good work ethic. Hard work will take you far. The following section will give you some helpful examples of how to improve by yourself and also with a partner.

Bear in mind that you are training to improve and make changes in your game. You must be very conscious of the fact that you are retraining your mind and body so that when you get into a match you can turn your brain off and just play without the distraction of thinking about the details of mechanics and court position. Now is the time to focus on the details; ingrain the right things into your brain, and teach your body the strokes, footwork, and proper responses to situations. If you make a mistake or do something wrong, do it over. Get it right. This type of discipline must be practiced.

One Person Drills

The Down the Line Pass

Drop and Hit

I know, I know, it's boring. But this is where it's at-- finding a reason to do the necessary work. The fact remains, if you can't control where you are hitting the ball, you can't win at the game of racquetball.

We are going to hit a <u>good</u> pass. Start the drill on the forehand side of the court. Set up so you are a little more than an arm and racquet's length away from the side wall. Begin with the proper forehand grip and start with the racquet back and ready to swing. You want all of your motion to be forward into the ball. Avoid starting with the racquet hanging down and making a loop back and then forward in one motion to hit the ball. This is a bad habit to get into during the rallies, and you certainly don't want to practice that way. Be sure that you drop the ball far enough away from you so that your elbow will be just short of locked at the point of contact. Start with a medium knee bend, your racquet up and your feet just less than shoulder width apart. Drop the ball even with your front foot. Now, stride parallel to the side wall and get the ball exactly in the middle of your stance. Be sure to keep the same height in your stance--don't drive up or dip down during the stroke. Swing and contact the ball about knee high and hit the shot <u>level</u> and straight in, parallel to the side wall.

Be diligent with your technique
during practice; this is where
your habits are formed.
Whether they are good or bad is
up to you.

The goal for this drill is to hit an effective pass. This means the ball will bounce first between the service line and the encroachment line, and bounce for the second time right in front of the ball wall. The ball should not touch the side wall or hit you during this drill.

Your goal is to have the ball travel to the front wall, *bounce on the short line*, and travel to the deep court without hitting the side wall. The shot should be hit no closer than six inches to the side wall; this will leave you some room for error.

Four reasons for doing this drill.

1. You must learn to control the flight and the path of the ball to its desired destination.
2. This is how your passes should be hit during the rallies; the path will carry the ball past your opponent in center court but not come off the back wall.
3. You want the height of the ball, the contact point, and the swing all to become automatic.
4. **A pass is not a left up kill**. This is "Old School" thinking in a new age of racquetball. Players are faster, equipment is better, and you cannot get away with that type of thought process any longer. Hit the shot you intend to hit.

Repeat the same drill on the backhand side, hitting the ball to the same place on the court. Be sure to start with the racquet back to ensure you are not making a loop with your stroke. Learn to control the down the line passes, they will become the basis of your game. This drill is very common because most players use it during the warm up period before they practice or play. Most players do not, however, pay much attention to where they are hitting the ball. Their only goal is to hit the ball between themselves and the wall they are facing. You should put more thought than that into the shot.

Practice your kill shots by moving up to the five foot line and killing the ball straight in. Make sure the ball does not hit the side wall at all and also bounces twice before the short line.

Feed and Hit

The next progression from this shot is to feed yourself a shot to the deep court on the forehand side. Hit the ball high and soft, making the second bounce behind the five foot line. This is more realistic practice because this is what happens during the games; the ball coming toward you and you practicing not only the stroke, but the timing of the stroke. Practice lining yourself up the proper distance away from the ball as soon as possible. This will allow you to move parallel to the side wall and into the shot. It is important that you first get comfortable with the mechanics of the swing, and then move into this drill. The goal is the same-- to hit the ball down the line, land the first bounce between the short line and the five foot line and bounce twice before the back wall.

For the backhand, the drill will be the same. The only exception would be that I would recommend you start with a forehand grip to feed yourself the shot. This will allow you to practice quickly switching from the forehand to the backhand grip. You do not have time to think about this during a match, so get comfortable with it now.

Always stride parallel to the side wall when hitting any forehand.

Note the extension of my arm and the height at which I contact this shot.

Be sure you practice letting the ball drop into your hitting zone as shown in the picture. The more often you do this, the more consistent you will be. Once you become proficient at these drills, add some variety to them by hitting short ceiling balls or balls that hit the side wall as your feed shots. Practice hitting the passes from all different situations and places on the court. Be sure you get the result you want. To track your progress, count how many good passes you can hit out of twenty balls. The definition of a good pass would be one that hits between the short line and the five foot line, does not hit the side wall and bounces twice before the back wall.

Off the Back Wall

To practice your footwork on shots off the back wall, feed yourself a shot off the back wall to the forehand side. At first, hit the ball hard enough to ensure it will carry out away from the back wall by a minimum of 10 feet. Position yourself about five feet away from the back wall to start. After you hit the feed shot, get the racquet up and establish the proper distance between yourself and the ball. As the ball goes by you, wait until it hits the back wall until you move forward. Make any lateral adjustments you need but wait for the ball to hit the back wall before moving forward. You do not want to get out ahead of the ball and be reaching back for it. This is a common error which creates lots of problems. Once the ball hits the back wall, time your stride so that you take a step and a half. Be sure to stride <u>parallel</u> to the side wall. The same rules apply to a shot off the back wall as they do to any other forehand--knees bent, good stride, shoulder and hips turn into the ball. Snap your wrist at impact and contact the ball directly in the middle of your stance to hit a down the line pass. Finish with good balance, knees bent, and a big follow through. Pick up the ball and repeat.

As you gain proficiency with this drill, hit your feed shot lower and softer off the back wall, making the shot more difficult. The closer you get to the back wall, the less of a stride forward you will take. Good racquet preparation is critical; if your racquet is touching the back wall and the ball is above eye level, let it come off the back wall, and hit the shot. If it is below eye level, hit a ceiling ball. This will help you develop a good decision-making process and not take stupid shots. Don't practice stupid shots either.

To make this practice drill more difficult, hit yourself ceiling balls until one of them comes off the back wall and shoot that one. This will help reinforce the decision-making process and be very similar to the shots you see in match play.

This line represents the back wall.

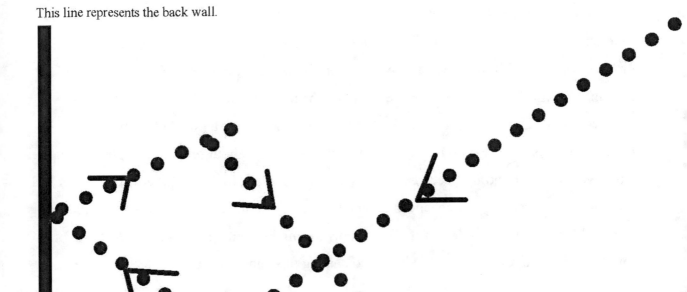

You want to be sure you end up behind the spot where the ball is going to bounce. This is so you can stride forward into the shot.

The key to getting consistent with shots off the back wall is to be sure you **get behind where to ball will end up,** and then move *toward* to front wall. Most people make the mistake of waiting where they think the ball will end up. The problem with this is twofold:

1   You have to guess perfectly every time.

2   You are not getting any momentum into the shot; so it will be hit with all arm.

Once again, start with a forehand grip to feed yourself the shot and then switch to a backhand grip. This will allow you to practice switching grips as well as hitting backhands off the back wall.

As you begin to get control over hitting the pass from off the back wall, begin to practice hitting kills from this position. Remember, don't aim in between and hope for a kill or hope for a pass, because they are two different shots. Be sure the pass hits behind the short line and the kills bounces twice before it. Avoid the in-between stuff, these shots are easily retrieved by your opponent. I typically don't recommend hitting a kill shot from this deep in the court unless you are a high level player. Contact the ball about mid-shin height and hit the ball level. This is important because if you take the ball waist high and hit down on it, not only are you increasing your chances of an error, but if you make the shot, the ball will rebound farther back into the court. This is only a matter of timing, so don't make the shot tougher or your opponent's job easier by contacting this shot too high.

You should also hit cross court passes and splats from each of the above situations with the exception of cross court kills. A cross court kill has to be perfect to work, and you don't want to *have* to be perfect to win. Practice your footwork and you will give yourself an easier shot to hit.

A good cross court pass will hit around the five foot line on the first bounce, and travel deep into the court on the side opposite from which you are standing. A wide angle pass will hit the side wall on the fly, hitting less than three feet high and traveling around the deep court towards the side it was hit from. This is a tough shot to hit consistently, so it will take some practice to make it a reliable shot. As stated before, the only difference in executing a cross court versus a down the line is to contact the ball earlier in your stance. Everything else is <u>exactly</u> the same.

Pinch Drills

When hitting pinches, remember that you do not want to hit the ball directly into the corner. Aim about two to three feet back on the side wall to create a better angle. This will help keep the ball farther forward in the court, making the ball bounce twice before the front service line. Contact the ball about mid-shin level to help avoid hitting the ball too high. Allowing it to drop to shoe-top level before swinging will likely result in a skip.

Drop and Hit drill

Again notice that my feet are square to the side wall, and not pointed at my target.

Observe the high racquet
preparation and the 45
degree step for my
backhand swing.

The ball is behind
my front foot in
order to create
the proper angle
for this shot.

This sounds too easy, but you want to practice striding at a 45 degree angle. Start by having your racquet back, and your left hand below your right arm. Drop the ball and then turn your shoulders back slightly, then pull with your upper body through the shot. The ball should be behind your front foot, giving you the proper angle to the corner. Remember, you will play the way you practice, so be diligent.

Practice this drop and hit drill from different locations in the court. The angles for the pinch are different depending on where you are standing, so practice from a variety of locations.

Rapid Fire Pinch Drill

OK, now for my favorite one. Stand between the service box and the five foot line. Drop the ball and hit a pinch into the forehand corner. Switch grips, square around, and hit a pinch into the backhand corner. Stay in this zone between the service box and the five foot line the entire time. Be sure to keep your feet in the proper position as much as possible. Switch grips and repeat, keeping the ball going regardless of the number of bounces. Avoid hitting reverse pinches. Keep this going as long as possible, until you make a mistake such as a skip or get forced into a reverse pinch. Stop and then start over. Be sure that you are getting the correct grip each time, don't settle for "close enough." Don't get into the habit of hitting the pinch high enough for the sake of continuing the drill. Be sure to put the shot away each time. It does not matter that the ball bounces more than once while doing this drill. Resist the tendency to point your feet to the direction of the shot you are hitting. This will alter your mechanics and also tip off your opponent where your next shot is going.

Another drill I like to practice is to hit ceiling balls (as many good ones as I can in a row) until I leave one either short or off the back wall, and then hit a down the line shot. In response to the down the line shot, I quickly prepare and hit a splat. I do this on both sides, focusing on hitting good shots on every opportunity. It develops your ceiling game, and teaches you to make good decisions in regards to when you should be aggressive. Do both forehands and backhands.

Also, hit an "around the wall" shot which hits side wall front wall, side wall all on the fly and travels deep into the court. This shot will provide you practice on balls that end up off the back wall as well as shots that come in short of the back wall. It develops the ability to judge when to be aggressive and when to wait for a better offensive opportunity. Do both forehands and backhands.

You can create all kinds of drills by combining the aforementioned drills. Another good one is to hit yourself a ceiling ball off the back wall, then hit a down the line pass. From that shot hit a splat, and then a cross court, starting the drill over after the cross court. Be sure not to leave the shots up for the sake of the drill, but rather disregard the number of bounces during this drill. Do this drill with both forehand and backhand. Be creative, and create drill that allow you to work on all parts of your game.

Two person Drills

Grab a partner for the next set of drills. It is not critical that you have a player of the same level to do drills with. If you can find someone else who is interested in doing drills with you, as long as they can hit the ball with any resemblance to consistency, you're in business.

My personal favorite--Assume good court position and have your practice partner stand in the backhand corner. They are going to hit you 25 splat shots and you are going to use the proper footwork and hit a down the line shot. Start with a forehand grip and good knee bend. Feet are shoulder width apart. Watch the ball leave your partner's racquet and develop the ability to quickly judge where that shot will end up. Your job is to move your right foot and then cross over with the left, lining up the shot and raising your racquet on the way to the ball. The shot to hit is down the line, so do it. Count how many good passes out of 25 you can hit.

From the same court position, now have your partner hit you 25 left-up Splats. Again, use the two step method, stepping with the right foot and then the left, moving forward into the service box. Kill the ball down the line and mix in some pinches but announce them first. Don't count your kills that hit the side wall as pinches. Count the results. Remember--feet shoulder width apart, good knee bend. Turn and watch the ball leave your partner's racquet and follow it until it leaves yours. Raise your racquet up as you go. The first step is the adjustment step.

We are simulating a very common scenario in this drill; my practice partner is hitting a shot from the left corner, and I am in my proper court position. He will hit splats, down the line, and cross court from this position so I can practice my footwork to each of these shots. My primary response is to hit my shot down the line, leaving me the most room for error.

This drill perfectly simulates what happens in a rally. You are **stopped** in the ready position, right foot touching the five foot line. Your opponent is in the deep court and is preparing to hit a shot. In a normal rally, you do not know what shot is coming, so do not cheat and start moving too soon.

Practice watching your opponent hit their shot, and learn to judge where the ball is going by seeing their contact point of the ball. If it is ahead of their front foot, that shot is probably going cross court.

Be as diligent as possible when practicing your footwork. You want to get to the point that you see your opponent hit a shot and run to the appropriate place on the court without thought. Train your instincts.

Now have your practice partner hit 25 backhands down the line. This is the toughest shot to cover, so don't be too surprised if you have difficulty with this shot at first. Ideally you want to hit the shot down the line again. The reason for this is that in a game situation your opponent will hit this shot and be charging into center court to cover the next shot. With this in mind, hitting down the line will make the ball travel away from your opponent. It will work if you end up hitting a good splat, but down the line has much more room for error in hitting a winner and therefore, it is the better choice.

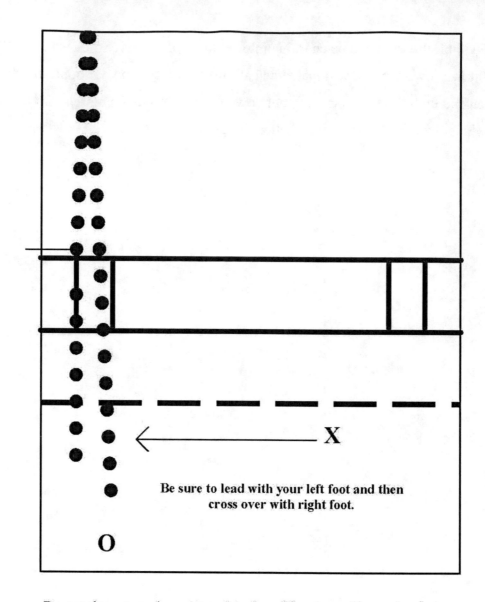

Be sure to lead with your left foot and then cross over with right foot.

X

O

Remember, you do not need to be offensive with every shot. If your opponent hits a good pass, be more conservative and hit a ceiling ball. You are better off resetting your good court position and continuing the rally than forcing a shot your not really set up for. If you go to the ceiling with a decent ceiling shot, the odds are still in your favor.

Serve and Return practice

Another good drill with your partner is to have him serve the same serve over and over and you practice making good decisions about the return. Your job, as the person receiving serve, is to make the correct decision as to be aggressive and shoot the ball or be patient and go to the ceiling. This is a critical skill for competitve play. The server should hit, for example, a Lob Nick Serve to the backhand. The server should strive to hit the serve as well as possible each time, not just throw it into play for you to hit. The returner's job is to get into proper position to return the ball effectively. The goal is to negate the server's advantage. If you make a bad choice and hit a splat off of that serve, you are giving points away. That shot is too difficult to make bounce twice in front of your opponent. If you cannot hit a pass, you are much better off going to the ceiling and waiting for a better opportunity.

Remember, you should make your opponent earn every one of his points. Don't take ill-advised shots and definitely don't ever skip a serve return.

A good way to do this drill is to have the server hit 20 serves to you and keep score. You get a point for hitting a pass or hitting a ceiling ball that does not give the server an offensive chance. The server gets a point by forcing you to hit a splat or hitting a bad ceiling ball. Switch after 20 and repeat. **Be sure to practice all the serves covered in the Serves section of the book.**

Section Summary-- Practice drills

--Be sure you are ready to drill. Don't muddle through practice sessions when tired or sick. You will only reinforce bad habits or sloppy play.

--Focus on the task at hand. Socialize after you're finished. Do your job.

--Decide in advance what shot you are going to work on, and do only that shot. If you are hitting kills, don't settle for passes thinking that will probably win anyway. It might, but don't settle.

--Practice getting the right distance away from the ball as soon as possible. Get the racquet back early, and be diligent with the footwork.

--Start with the simple drills and work your way up to the more difficult ones. Understanding and being consistent with the basics is very important to success.

--Pay close attention to your form at all times. Be sure you are replacing the old you with the new you that you want to become. If you practice lazily, that is how you will play.

--Chart your progress. Be sure you're gaining ground--it will help keep you excited about practicing and moving towards your goals.

--Videotape yourself for occasional review.

Match Play

Managing the Flow of a Match

It has come to my attention that a lot of players think the server has all the advantages. This is true only in the sense that most players do not utilize the things that are written in the rules for them. Here are a few examples:

As the receiver, you have 10 seconds after the referee calls the score to prepare. You can hold your racquet up and delay the start of the next rally. Learn to be conscious of the pace at which the server is comfortable, and try to avoid their comfort zone. Strive to slow the fast paced, serve and shoot style players by raising your racquet often before serves. There is nothing better than having your opponent hit a good serve at you only to realize you had been standing there with your racquet in the air. Some players are very much affected by this practice, and they will grow very agitated if you persist. It is perfectly legal and well within the rules for the receiver to do this after *every* rally if they choose to do so.

Do not let someone run a bunch of points in a row without some sort of disruption. Racquetball is a game of momentum and uninterrupted momentum (your opponent's) can be a dangerous thing. Ask the referee a question like "How many time-outs do I have left in this game?" A lot of players will kind of let down if they think you are going to call time-out. Do a good job of selling the fact that you might call it--turn and face the door, maybe reach for the door handle, etc., and then turn around to receive serve. Trust me, this works. You must employ this at the right time and only once in a match. Save it for the tie-breaker or close game; don't waste it in a blowout situation and reduce the effect if you get the chance to use it later on. **If you lose a game and still have time-outs left, you have mis-managed that game**.

It is difficult to speed up the pace of play if you are playing a slow and deliberate player.

Luckily, most players fall into the other category. You can log a few complaints to the ref if they are truly taking too long but other than that there is little you can do. The best way to combat this is to become comfortable playing at the slower pace and then the flow of a match always will be within your control.

When you are in the service box, be aware of what your opponent is doing and feeling, in addition to your own thoughts. If you made them dive twice in the last rally and they are sucking wind, try to start the next rally as soon as possible. Maybe even be willing to forego your usual rituals to gain the edge in these situations. Obviously, if they hold up their racquet to delay you, you must comply. But not everyone will do that. I love to force the pace, knowing that I have trained and prepared for this level of physical output and can outlast just about anyone in a cardiovascular duel. Start the rally and make them run again. Repeat this process as often as possible; the cumulative effect on your opponent will be obvious. If you are using the principles in this book, your opponent should be working harder than you are anyway, so the more you can add to that the better.

If your opponent hits a bad shot or gets a bad call, you should do one of two things. If your opponent is someone who is dwelling on the bad shot or arguing with the ref about the call, let them go. Very few people are doing themselves a favor by focusing on the past and not getting ready for the next rally. The opposite is of course to force the pace and restart the action as soon as possible. You may find your opponent will take out their anger by swinging a lot harder in the rally following a bad call and thus, make more errors. Your opponent's

venting during the next rally usually will benefit you. Learn how to control the flow of a match and use this to your advantage. It is an invaluable skill and can make your job on the court.

知识就是力量

Knowledge is Power

Using Your Time-Outs Effectively

It drives me crazy to watch a match and never see either player call a time out. I can't believe how little this opportunity is utilized. To reiterate an important thought from earlier in the book, **"If you lose a game and still have any time outs left, you have mis-managed that game."**

If you are someone who does not focus well for long periods of time, I would recommend breaking up a 15 point game into two or three stages. By breaking the game at least in half, if not into three parts, it is much easier to stay intensely focused. It is easier to stay focused for these short periods of time than to spread that focus over the whole game.

Use your time outs for the following eight reasons:

1. To break your opponent's momentum.

2. To recover after a really long rally.

3. To keep yourself properly hydrated. Drink **water** during any break in the match.

4. To give yourself an extra moment to collect your thoughts, evaluate your current strategy, and decide what you want to do the next couple of points.

5. To discuss your opponent's court position, serve patterns, etc., with a coach or friend in the crowd.

6. Check your equipment. Make sure your shoes are clean on the bottom (especially if you are playing on a slick court). Fix your strings to help prevent premature breakage. Clean your glasses of any sweat or fingerprints.

7. Change gloves if your grip is starting to slip.

8. Change shirts if yours is soaked with perspiration.

Obviously, take advantage of your own momentum. Don't call a time out when you are running points on your opponent. If they call time-out, use it to accomplish the things listed above. I don't like the idea of staying on the court and "practicing" your swing or a new serve. You should have done that before the tournament and you are not going to learn something new during a 60 second time-out. If your opponent begins to catch on to your serving patterns or shots, or you feel yourself getting distracted or needing a mental break, then use one of your time outs.

Do not wait until your opponent gets to 14 to call time-out. This is very predictable (boringly so) and will not really catch your opponent off guard if they expect you to call it. Call your time out at 13.

Four Reasons for calling a Time Out at 13 (or 9):

1. You give yourself some margin for error. You now have room to go for a shot without the worry of handing the game away at 14 (or 10).
2. You will usually catch your opponent off guard by calling your time-out at 13 (or 9).
3. If you lose the rally at 13, you still have another chance to get the serve back. Your opponent may get tentative or they may force a shot trying to end it too soon.
4. You need to formulate a plan for when you get back into the service box. How far down are you? Are you within striking distance or should you "go for broke" to try and overcome a big deficit.

Welcome to the Zone

These are the days for which athletes live.

It happens to everyone who plays any sport at least once in his athletic lifetime; the athlete finds himself **"in the Zone"**. Everything is beautiful here, everything you touch--golden. Moments like these are why most of us stay in an athletic pursuit. Once you've had a taste, you will always long for another. To be in the zone, to be one with the moment, is an awesome human experience.

I have been fortunate enough to have played entire matches in the Zone. The experience is phenomenal; the court seems smaller and I feel bigger than I really am. It seems the ball is moving slower and I always know where my opponent is standing. I react without thought, accept things without judgment and have instant knowledge of every situation. There is total silence, inside my head and out. This feeling is why I play racquetball.

One of my most memorable "Zoned" matches was a finals match at the Northern Arizona Racquetball Championships in Flagstaff. I was working toward that tournament, and particularly the finals, for about six months. I knew my time had come, I was ready to win. Ironically, I played poorly in the doubles final immediately before the singles finals. I had come there to win the singles finals and I clicked into the Zone at 0-0 in the first game and never came out of it until I got in the shower after the match. I beat Pat Gonzales in four games and played one of the best matches of my life. Almost every match I have played against Pat in the Open division has been close, usually resulting in tie-breakers. But that day, I was larger than life, and it was the greatest feeling in the world. I can't even put into words how awesome matches like that are. To this day, I remember that match and draw

upon that experience for motivation. Moments like that are yours forever.

One of the hardest things about the Zone is staying there. It is tough enough to find your way into the Zone but I think staying there is even tougher. The slightest thing can snap you out of it-- for example getting too excited about a particular shot, a bad call, a time-out, someone in the crowd telling you how great you are playing, etc. Staying out of your own way is sometimes very difficult. Learning to control your thoughts and manage yourself regardless of what happens in a match is a skill that comes only with practice in those situations and effective visualization before your matches. Establishing consistent rituals and routines to use during a match are critical to keeping yourself in the Zone.

知识就是力量

Knowledge is Power

Routines and Rituals

If you can establish a good routine before each serve and return, this will help you stay present-minded and focused on the next shot. Dwelling on the last one will not accomplish anything. These rituals need to be practiced constantly, and cannot be compromised regardless of the situation. The most obvious ritual in the game of racquetball was demonstrated by US Open Champion Jason Mannino. If you have ever watched him play, you know to what I am referring to. Before every serve Jason takes the ball, bounces it on the floor behind the front service line making it bounce into the front wall. He then hits the ball sidewall-frontwall-sidewall and catches it before it hits the floor. Next he pulls the wrist lacer tight on his wrist and is now ready to serve. I have never talked to Jason about this, but I assume he is thinking about what serve he wants to hit and what he is going to do next. He is controlling the tempo of the match, and is going to serve when he is ready. This is a good way to collect your thoughts, catch your breath, think about the serve you want to hit and prepare for the next rally. Be a little more original then to just copy what Jason does. Create your own rituals and use them to your advantage. Be sure you you are ready to serve within the allotted 10 seconds after the rally.

When returning serve, I like to use my rituals but allow room for altering them if necessary, because I may want to change the pace of the match as I feel appropriate. I can dictate the pace between points as I want. If I think it is better to have the serve come to me right away, I won't hold up my racquet and delay the server. If the situation is tight and I want the server to think about it, then I hold up my racquet or walk around the service return area. I want the serve to come when **I** feel most prepared. I try to establish control of the pace from the beginning and keep it throughout the match.

After every rally, this is what goes through my mind:

1   **Did I or my opponent dive during the last rally?**
               —— **if yes, check the floor for dangerous sweat spot. If no, go to #2.**
2   **Gain control of my breathing. I want to be sure I am physically ready to play the next rally.**
3   **Should I force the pace of play or take my time?**
4   **Check my strings. Make sure they are in place.**
5   **Tell myself to "hit a smart return" or picture *exactly* what serve I want to hit.**
6   **Take position to return serve or set up to execute my next serve.**

Understanding what someone else is thinking is difficult, especially when there are a lot of other things to monitor during a match. This is why you should practice your rituals all the time and make them an automatic response in these situations. Then you can scratch that off your list of things to think about while you're playing. Don't give yourself a long list of instructions before each play--it's too much to think about. I like to limit my thoughts to general concepts like "hit a good pass." Avoid being too general, like thinking "just hit the front wall". This is too vague a command for your body to follow.

Remind yourself during the rallies to watch the ball. The only other thing to add is to pay attention to what your opponent is doing. I don't mean micro-managing every little reaction they have. I'm talking about noticing when they are out of breath from a hard rally, upset at a bad call or a hinder, etc. Don't spend too much time on them; after all, this is only a supplement to a good game plan, not the focus of it. I don't want you to think I'm encouraging trash talking or distracting your opponent. That is not good sportsmanship, and ultimately not how you want to win.

Using rituals under pressure will help to keep you focused and present- minded. Running through your rituals before serving or returning serve may help to relieve some of the pressure you are experiencing during the match. Professional tennis players all have clear cut rituals which they follow religiously and can be copied and put to use for yourself. Remember that tennis players have at least 30 seconds between each point, so you will need to trim their rituals to fit racquetball's 10 seconds. Find things that are helpful, such as fixing your strings while you're thinking of your next serve or return. Avoid looking into the gallery between points. Stay focused on the task at hand, not on who is watching you play.

There is no substitute for real life practice for your rituals. Tournament play is where it counts, so play and learn and appreciate those who bring the best out in you.

Appreciate Your Rivals

During my run from a low Open player to the Pro Tour, I had many an epic battle with Pat Gonzales. He had some good wins over some well known players, including some Touring Pros. I'm fairly sure Pat has beaten me more times than not overall, but I had the good fortune to win the last seven finals we played. I used Pat as a great source of motivation. When I was tired, I would remind myself that Pat was at the club practicing. I would come to the club on Sunday nights to practice, thinking I was one practice session ahead of him for the week. In a four year span Pat and I played in six finals and one semi-finals, and we were so evenly matched that most of the matches went to the fifth game and were decided by two points. Two Points! After two hours of play it would come down to two points. This was a great learning experience for me. It taught me how to perform under pressure. It taught me to never stop trying to find ways to win. I also learned to weather the storm, and hang around long enough to get into position to win. Regardless of how tired I was, how badly I needed a weekend off, I could get motivated to play Pat. I learned a lot about myself through our rivalry. I have learned to respect him as a person and a player and for all of these things, I am grateful. Thanks, Pat.

If you have the good fortune of having someone very close to your ability and you face frequently, use that scenario for all it offers. The competitive spirit and the mutual help you are giving one another are all invaluable. Learn to appreciate this relationship; don't let your desire to win outweigh good sportsmanship or common courtesy. Do your best to handle these situations as well as possible; learn from your mistakes and grow, personally and athletically. Take it from me, years from now when you are looking back on all of this, you do not want any regrets. "There is no pillow as soft as a clear conscience." (Lao Tzu)

Breathing

Professional tennis players do a noticeable job of staying present when playing matches. They have a very set pattern of rituals they always follow. Staying in the present begins with your breathing. Dr. James Loehr is a well respected sports psychologist dealing mainly with tennis players. Every player he works with learns to develop control over their breathing as one of their rituals to rely upon under pressure.

In my opinion, there are very few good examples of this in the game of professional racquetball. Players *are* doing things to assist them in staying focused, but the rituals appear to be somewhat random and far less noticeable then tennis players. On the racquetball court, it is easy to tell who is winning and who is losing. Not only do most racquetball players do a poor job of showing how to play the game properly, but very few players are adept at using rituals under pressure.

You must take control of your breathing. When you have a long rally or are very nervous and begin to breathe through your mouth, you activate the "fight or flight" response in your brain. Your brain has put your body into survival mode. Things like swinging smoothly and moving freely become secondary to thoughts of getting enough oxygen into your system. This is a response at the deepest level of human existence and everyone goes through this process when competing in an athletic endeavor.

First, you must learn to recognize this occurrence, otherwise you cannot deal with it properly. Once you begin to catch on to this when it occurs, you can nip the panic response in the bud. Breathe in through the nose, pushing your stomach *out* as you inhale. **Yes, I said *out* as you**

inhale. This will suck the air to the bottom of your lungs where it is most readily absorbed into your bloodstream. Exhale by expelling the used air out through your mouth and pulling your bellybutton in towards your spine. This is the most efficient way to breathe. Not only does this get more oxygen into your system more efficiently, you are also in control of your breathing. This, in turn, leads to controlling your thoughts, emotions and actions on the court. If you can avoid triggering that fight or flight response, you will be more presented-minded for the task at hand.

A good way to practice this is to lie on the floor face up and put a heavy book on your belly button. The idea is to push the book up towards the ceiling as you inhale and get the feel of the weight of the book "squishing" the air out of you as you exhale.

Never start another rally without regaining control of your breathing and your heart rate. If you train properly, you should be able to gain control over your breathing within the 20 seconds you have between the end of the rally and the start of the next. (I know the rule says 10 seconds, but I say 20 seconds because realistically you can meander back to the return area and then hold your racquet up, thereby extending the time you have.) Your heart rate should drop considerably in this time. If you are very fit, you have the advantage in these situations. If you are capable of pushing the pace over and over, and not have it be detrimental to your game, you can add this to your list of weapons for tournament play. Bear in mind, if you do not possess a high degree of fitness, this may work against you. Play within your own abilities. If you cannot keep that fast pace up for a whole match, slow things down and play at a pace you can handle. Don't do things that are going to work against you.

Centering Yourself

This is an invaluable skill. When I did some martial arts training, I was fortunate enough to be taught a skill that I have used frequently during tournament play. It is called "Centering." Concentrate on the spot two inches below your navel. This is the exact center of your body (for 90% of the population). After a long rally, take a huge breath in through the nose. Expand you chest and push your stomach out as you inhale. Blow the breath out through your mouth with a loud *whew* sound. With practice, you will be able to recover your breathing to a normal rate even after strenuous exercise with this one breath. This practice will help to keep you present-minded and focused. You must practice this diligently to be able to use this technique.

This is important if you like to force the pace in a match. I used this technique over and over, with great success, and outlasted most of my opponents after back-to-back long rallies. When you tire someone out, even if is temporary, they become mistake-prone. As the saying goes "Fatigue makes cowards of us all". Of course, you must have a good fitness base to draw from, otherwise it probably won't work. It may help to push with your fingertips gently on this spot to remind you of the exact spot to concentrate on. This is the power source of your whole body. If you focus on this spot, you are giving yourself something specific to think about. If you have specific questions about this technique, you may want to consult an accomplished martial artist or Yoga instructor.

Another Type of Breathing

When you watch other people play matches, you may notice that some of them hold their breath when they hit the ball. There is a delicate balance, because you want to exhale as you swing, but if you are holding your breath, you are likely to be flexing your midsection as you swing. This will impede your rotation and shorten up your follow-through. Try to be relaxed and smooth as you swing, not flexing so hard that you are tiring yourself out and impeding your natural swing.

I am a big believer in using your breathing to help you hit your shots with *resolve.* Exhaling as I hit my shots helps me be very focused at that moment. My eyes get bigger and are focused solely on the ball, I inhale just before I begin my swing and exhale as I "let 'er rip" with my swing. It is *resolved*-- clean, pure, and totally in the moment. There should be no thoughts in your mind other than the shot you are hitting.

A great idea to improve overall health, learn to breathe correctly, and add to your flexibility is to check into a Yoga class. Your health club may offer a program, or you may need to go to another facility to receive this training. A word of advice--start at the beginning class regardless of how fit or athletic you think you are. It is substantially harder than you might think.

知识就是力量

Knowledge is Power

Something to Consider...

If you know your opponent really well (for example, you play this person in tournaments frequently), be sure you notice what pace they are most comfortable with. I know that some players I faced were very tough to deal with when allowed to play at their own pace. These players are rhythm players and they thrive on the fast-paced action. Be flexible in your approach to the pace of the match. Be sure you can play effectively at a fast pace which forces the action and pushes the fitness level, but also be able to play slowly and methodically. If you slow that person down between rallies, stall within the limits of the rules, and basically drag things out, you may find things are totally different for that player. I have discussed some of my favorite ways to slow things down in a match in the Managing the flow of a match section in this book. Feel free to plagiarize my work or come up with your own material. Either way, it is important that you can play comfortably at both speeds, so you can force the pace or slow things down and make your opponent miserable.

Match Management

It's not personal--what really happened vs. your interpretation.

This is a tough one. This skill is probably the most difficult at which to excel, let alone think about mastering. It has happened to all of us. The match is close, 5-5 in the tiebreaker, and after a long rally you hit a flat roll down the forehand line. You know it was good and the crowd reacts accordingly. You pump your fist, give it a little *yeah!* and start walking to the service box to serve out the match. Only then do you realize the referee has called your shot a skip.

Option 1. You go berserk, yelling obscenities at the referee about him and his mother, and begin banging your racquet on the nearest hard surface.
Option 2. You turn to your opponent and call him a cheater for taking that terrible call and remind him that what goes around comes around.
Option 3. You control your breathing and your reaction, accept the call and formulate a plan to get the serve back.

Lord knows that we all have been guilty of choosing option 1 in far too many situations. It is the easiest one, you vent your frustrations on the source of the problem--the referee. You're mad about winning the rally and having the referee disagree with you. Yelling and screaming will get you nothing, trust me on this. You will not be able to intimidate anyone into giving the next close call to you. It does not really work that way. If anything, you are probably talking the ref into <u>never</u> giving <u>you</u> a <u>call</u> again <u>for</u> the <u>rest</u> of <u>your</u> natural <u>life.</u>

Option 2 is no good either. You are likely to play this person again, or worse yet, have them as a referee in the future. The last thing you want to do is make enemies and cause problems for yourself in the future.

Option 3 is the right choice-- the professional choice, the choice of the person who is calm and collected, prepared for the worst and surprised by nothing. Emotional detachment is difficult but necessary. I don't expect you not to react at all, but you need to limit your reaction and get over it very quickly. Get back to focusing on the task at hand. This skill must be practiced, every single match you play. Daily life certainly affords you plenty of practice opportunities. Each situation is different and will test you every time it occurs. You will gain nothing by freaking out during the situation. You must remain calm and do what you came here to do.

Center yourself. This is the only way to prevail. Try to delay your reaction to what happened and realize it is not personal, it is just what happened. If you can learn to appreciate this, it will carry you a long way.

It is easy to overturn a call while winning big or getting killed. This is not something out of the ordinary. In the spirit of good sportsmanship, you should overturn calls regardless of the score. It is the true measure of your integrity. Overturning a call at 9-9 in the tie-breaker--that is extraordinary. You should have the confidence to win the right way--the fair way-- especially if you find yourself on the flip side of the above situation. People will respect you and you will develop a reputation for being a fair player. Your negative reputation will grow three times as quickly if you take the other route.

Don't try that at home

It's great to go to a Professional tournament and watch the best players in the world do their thing. I would watch Marty Hogan, Cliff Swain, Sudsy Monchik, Andy Roberts, Mike Yellen, John Ellis, and the other top players play in tournaments I attended. I was trying to learn what areas to attack, what things to look for when I would play them, etc. One thing I learned quickly was that some of the top players hit shots and did things I was not capable of doing. I saw Sudsy jump *up* and roll a backhand splat from 39 feet deep, not once but twice in a match at the US Open. I also watched John Ellis go into the right corner, run two steps up the back wall, spin in a circle and hit a backhand down the right wall. Unbelievable. I once saw Tim Doyle misread a shot he thought was going to be a forehand, spin in a circle away from the front wall and flat roll a backhand. Absolutely amazing! Jason Mannino amazes crowds with his diving gets, Shane Vanderson impresses with eyeball high backhand splats that roll out, and on and on. Kane Waselenchuk has the fastest hands I've ever seen, and hits shot that literally no one else could hit. However, I did not try to incorporate these things into my game; they are too hard to do. If I could do those things, I, too, would be one of the top five players in the world.

The message I am trying to convey is that these players all have very solid foundations from which this sort of play comes. For example, Sudsy has worked with Ruben Gonzales since he was about six years old. If his basic racquetball skills weren't as good as they are, he would not be able to play to the level he has achieved. Every one of the top Pros is very consistent with the *basics* of the game. They did not start out hitting shots like that; they all but mastered the *basics* of the game and then ventured out of the normal ranges. Don't think, if you can't consistently hit a down the line pass from knee high, that you should start practicing a shoulder high splat because the best players can hit that shot. Stay within your ability when you are playing matches. It will take you much farther than trying shots you are not really capable of executing.

One of the things you should try to do when watching some of the pros play is to look for things like good footwork and focusing on the ball. Many of the pros do have very good footwork, but there are exceptions. You want to model yourself after players who do the fundamentals well, not those who have excelled with a unique style. It is likely someone with a unique style, that is an Open or Pro level player, is athletically talented and is getting by more on physical talent than solid fundamentals. Admire them if you like, but don't emulate their game.

Visualization

This is an important skill. You must develop the capacity to see things in your mind before you are about to do them. It is a dress rehearsal for the events to come. You can work through most of the situations you will face in your first final, your first out of town tournament match, whatever the case may be. There are a lot of books on the market about this topic, and I would recommend that you get some of them and learn the art of visualization. This skill, just like any other, gets better with practice. I will share some things I did to get you started.

One thing I found very helpful was to remember an experience that I had already had. This is very similar to visualizing, but probably easier because you already lived that experience. Think back to a good or bad experience that happened to you. Try to feel what you were feeling at that time. Picture yourself in the situation. Imagine the surrounding noises, smells, etc. Remember what you were wearing. It is important to recall as much detail as possible-- the more vivid, the better. I'll give you an example:

The tournament I consider my breakthrough event was held here in Arizona. I always thought that once you could win tournaments in your state, it was time to venture out to the bigger events. As I had previously discussed, it was the Northern Arizona Racquetball Championships. I played Pat Gonzales in the finals of that event. I had worked long and hard toward that match. I knew I was ready. When I think back to that match, I still get goose bumps almost instantly. I remember what I was wearing for that match; I had saved my favorite shirt for the finals. The floor has the club's logo in light blue in the service box. There is a big space between the floor and the left side wall from the front wall all the way to the back. The floor creaks in the front right corner when you walk on it. The court is slightly below the main floor of the club; the side wall is glass from the club floor to the ceiling, with panel from knee level to the floor of the court. The carpeting is dark, and people are sitting literally right next to the glass side wall.

I felt bigger than I really am; the court seemed small that day. I knew going into the match that I was going to get to nearly every ball Pat hit. My breathing was calm and deep. I had on a brand new glove and it fit perfectly. I put on new socks and saved my favorite headband for the match. At the start of the match, I walked forward and put my hands on the front wall. I remember feeling a surge of electricity run through me. It was my time to shine. I remember standing in the service box looking into the glass and seeing my reflection. I couldn't see perfect detail but I remember thinking that I looked big, focused and confident. The court was the perfect temperature. The high altitude of Flagstaff got to my opponent that day but I felt winded only after the longest rally of the match (I dove four times in that rally). I was so energized it was as if I was vibrating.

I still get that same tingling feeling when I close my eyes and recall that situation. I have called upon that feeling many times to get myself into the proper frame of mind to compete.

Before I had this experience to draw from, I used to picture other people playing in pressure situations. There was a player in Arizona who was good in the clutch , and I would picture myself as him. I knew that he would not miss shots in those situations. Over time, I realized that I was, in fact, the one who had come through in the clutch and could now start to picture *myself* doing the things necessary to win.

Imagery

The main difference between imagery and visualization is that visualization is a third person view of an event. When you learn to use imagery, you are picturing yourself in a situation and are mentally "experiencing" things which you want to improve or prepare.

To the body, Imagery is the more powerful of the two. The reason for this is the brain will send physical and chemical signals to the appropriate muscles when you are mentally rehearsing something. It is very similar to actually experiencing the event. This is a very useful tool when you are preparing for your first final, your first tournament match, or anything that you have not already experienced. You can prepare yourself for the upcoming event and lessen your nerves or rehearse your responses in advance, and be better prepared to handle the event.

As discussed in the previous section, "feeling" the experience is critical to mentally rehearsing the events about to come. Imagery is the ability to think and feel what has not been experienced yet. In my mind, I have defeated many players who are better than myself. I also have hit holes in one and hit the winning three point shot from half court to win the finals. I have yet to actually do any of these, but I already know basically what it feels like to do them.

Goal setting

You must define what you want to accomplish. Whether you want to win a National Championship or the "C" division league at the Club Championship next fall, you must have a plan of action to help you achieve that goal.

A person with great dreams can achieve great things.

There are many good books available on goal setting. I would recommend finding one to suit your needs. My near maniacal approach to goal setting may not be suited for most people. As a coach, I would not let *any* of my students follow in my exact footsteps. (Hindsight is 20/20).

Here are some basic suggestions are as follows:

1. Have a very lofty goal as a long term goal. By long term I mean 3 to 5 years away. This would be an ultimate personal achievement.
2. Set intermediate goals of one year. Pick a tournament or two that you want to do well in or maybe win.
3. Pick some reachable short term goals. I would recommend having some of these goals be non "result-oriented" such as practicing 15 days in the next month or adding an off-court training program to your routine.
4. Reward yourself for the goals you accomplish; reset the ones you do not. If you did not reach a goal, ask yourself why. If you wanted to win the club championships but were sick that week, maybe that's not your fault. Or, was it psychosomatic? Adjust your

goals and training accordingly. If you find yourself habitually sick during tournaments, seek a psychologist. If you win the club championship, celebrate for a week and then pick a new goal. If you have no defined goals, you will have difficulty moving forward.

Bear in mind, the future is what dictates what you will become. I believe the past has nothing to do with the future. If you can picture a different set of circumstances for yourself in the future, whether it is becoming more fit or having a better job, that goal can help you change the present. You must realize that goal setting can be approached this way, and not get stuck in the mindset of, "Well, I'm just going to learn to live with the way things are." Make it happen by setting the goal and letting it pull you forward and direct your life into that new reality.

"I thought I looked

better than that"

--every one of my students

Videotaping your matches.

Brace yourself because you are about to see the naked truth about your racquetball game. This is not the distorted view that we all see in our heads, this is the real thing. Set up a video camera and tape a practice session, practice match or a tournament match. Then set aside some time to review the tape and take some notes. Be sure you do this little project when you have a few weeks before your next tournament. You will need time to work on the things that are weak or lacking in your game. How are your strokes? Are you in good court position? Are your knees bent during the rallies? Did you skip more forehands than backhands? Did you make a bunch of serve return errors? Did you lose rallies due to poor shot selection? There are a myriad of things to look at and work on, and working on any of them will bring you closer to your goals as a player. Once you look at the video and learn what you need, file the tape away for review at a later date. Avoid sitting and watching yourself do things incorrectly over and over. It will only ingrain the habit further. Look at it once, take notes and put it away. Six months from now, watch it again to remind yourself how far you've come. Suck it up, be honest and critical, and learn from your mistakes.

Time to Take your Skills on the Road

Traveling to Out of Town Tournaments

When you venture off to an out of town tournament, there are several things you need to take into consideration:

1. **Always show up to the tournament a day early.** You will benefit greatly by showing up a day early and getting familiar with your surroundings. It is good to check into the hotel, find a grocery store, and buy whatever supplies you may need for the stay. I like to have food available in the hotel room; I always eat more, and more often, during tournaments. Next, go to the club and practice to get a feel for the speed of the courts on which you are going to play. Check the draw sheets yourself and verify your starting time. Get familiar with the layout of the club. Know where the locker rooms are, if you need to bring a lock, and find out if you need to smuggle a towel out of the hotel. Introduce yourself to the Tournament Director; this may be the only person who can help you with any problems that may occur.

2. **Travel is hard on the body.** Any time you sit in the same position for an extended period of time, your muscles tighten. If you are stuck in the car behind the wheel, it seems as though the energy is drained right out of you. It is mentally draining to drive a long distance, especially in traffic. It is worse if you are running late and are trying to "make up time". Even though you are not physically active at that time, your legs will seem heavy and slow. This is not going to help you get through your first round match. You should be focused on the task at hand, not on the details of finding a hotel and the like. Flying is sometimes even worse than a long drive. Being trapped on an airplane in those small seats, breathing the same air everyone else is breathing, being

dehydrated by the air conditioning systems and eating the poor food which airlines provide is not conducive to playing your best.

To combat these problems, do a few simple things such as bring a bottle of water on the plane with you. Carry a small bag to hold the water, some fruit or nuts, a book, and my Ipod. Keeping your mind occupied during the trip is a good way to avoid feeling so drained upon arrival. I think its best not too eat most of the food served on the plane, so I try to eat before and after my flight and snack on something healthy during the flight. I wear a warm-up suit because I find that is the most comfortable thing I can wear; it is warm enough to wear when the plane is cold and, if I take off the jacket, I am in just a T-shirt and pants. Your sponsor will also appreciate you walking through the airport wearing their clothing.

3. Time Zone Changes. If you travel to an earlier time zone, you will have to deal with the difference in time and how your body feels at certain times of the day. Most of us are not used to playing a match at 5:00 AM, but if you have an 8:00 AM match on the east coast and you live in Arizona, it will feel that way. Can you play well enough to win? The best way to combat the effects of time changes is the get to the club early and get a very good warm-up ride, run, swim, or whatever you need to do the lose the "morning fuzziness" and be ready to play.

4. Details. Be sure to take care of things like having a ride to the club. If you flew into town and do not have a car, does the hotel have a shuttle service? Does it use a set schedule or can you call the front desk and have them take you right away? You do not want to rush into the club five minutes after your scheduled starting time and have to shorten your warm up time. You will be stressed out before even getting onto the court, and that is not how you want to start the match.

By showing up early, you can take care of all the little details that need to be dealt with and get settled into your temporary new home. Focus on winning the upcoming match; this is where your energy should be spent.

Nutrition

There are many schools of thought and thousands of diet books on this subject. Most of them are better used as a fire-starter than a way to live your life. Eat a sensible diet that is balanced well with clean protein, good carbohydrates, and some good fat. Radical diets are hard on your system and are destined to fail. You need to think, in the long term, about changing your body structure. View it as a lifestyle change, not a temporary diet. This is the best way to get results. Every cell in your body will be replaced by this time next year, and the entire blood supply is replaced in three to four months. In six months, all of the proteins in your body die and are replaced, even the DNA in your genes. In a year, everything including your bones and even the enamel in your teeth is replaced, constructed entirely of the nutrients that you eat. If you have a coffee and Twinkies diet, you'll get a coffee and Twinkies body. As an athlete, you have very little room to stray from the path. You must realize your time is limited and live your life accordingly. Read **Optimum Sports Nutrition** by Dr. Michael Colgan. It is one of the most informative and scariest books you will ever read.

When I was training and playing full time, I worked with a nutritionist and got some good advice about what to eat. I also learned when to eat, which can be just as critical. Remember, I am 5'7" and was about 132 pounds at that time, with a super-charged metabolism and a busy schedule. I have not included my diet plan because it would not be appropriate for most to follow. But consulting a sports nutritionist was a huge help for me, and I am sure it would help you as well.

During a tournament, my diet schedule had to change because of the varied schedule and time spent on the court. I usually played singles and doubles at local tournaments, or Pro's and Open at the IRT events. This means a lot of court time; so I needed to be smart and flexible about what and when I ate. During a tournament I typically tried to consume as much or more than I usually do compared to non-tournament weeks. Tournament Racquetball takes its toll on the body and mind. I knew I needed food to fuel myself for the matches during the weekend. **Flexibility is the key to life.** Don't fall into the trap of having to stick to a set routine to feel "normal".

***Remember that you cannot clean up your diet two days before a tournament and expect to get optimum results. A healthy lifestyle is important for general well-being and critical to athletic success.

Water

Water is a big key to top performance. Drink distilled water in huge quantities--a gallon a day, at least. Your body cannot function and recover without it. When preparing for a tournament, you should be sure to drink a gallon of water the day *before* your first match, and a gallon of water the day of your match. You may find that during the weekend of the tournament you will want more than a gallon of water during the day. Listen to your body; if you wait until you are thirsty to begin drinking, you can be upwards of 30% dehydrated. Proper muscle function will decrease at as little as 10% dehydration, so if you feel thirsty at any time during a match, your muscles are not functioning at their optimum levels. Obviously your performance level is intricately timed to your body's ability at that moment, so be sure to be well prepared.

DO NOT drink sports drinks or worse yet energy drinks during your matches. Provided you are reasonably nourished, your body is in electrolyte overload during exercise, so you do not need to worry about replacing electrolytes yet. If you were a triathlete, it would be a different story. The second reason you should not consume sports drinks during your matches is the fact that most of the sports drinks on the market contain a lot of sugar. This will drastically slow the absorption rate of water into your body. You will never catch up with the body's demand for clean, pure water if you drink anything other than water during your match.

After your match, and <u>after</u> drinking another 32 ounces of water, that is the time for an electrolyte drink. This is the time your body needs to replace the glycogen in the system; so what you eat and drink after your matches is just as important as what you eat before.

Rest and Sleep

The athletes who are short of sleep, or sleep poorly, are the first to succumb to injury and burnout. Body growth and repair takes place only during sleep. For hard-training athletes, eight hours a night plus a nap in mid-afternoon will be a huge help in aiding growth, repair and recovery. I realize this is not easy for most people to accomplish, so be sure to get plenty of sleep as often as possible. If you can to the tournament to party and have a good time, don't worry about it. If you can to win…GET A GOOD NIGHT'S SLEEP!!!!

Successful development of an athlete is a delicate balance of three things: a variable training strength training program as well as a good practice schedule, the correct raw materials to maintain and repair mind and muscle, and sufficient sleep to permit repair and growth to take place. **The best thing you can do to improve as an athlete is to stay healthy so you may practice and train.**

Hopefully you do not have trouble sleeping during tournaments. If you are too worked up the day before a match, be sure to get a light workout in during the day. This should help you fall asleep faster. Also, reading just before your go to sleep, or listening to some relaxing music as you fall asleep can do the trick. I would recommend avoiding sleeping pills because they can leave you groggy the following morning. If you do have a problem with sleeping, get it figured out as soon as possible. You need the rest to recover from the day's matches.

Preparing for Tournaments

How to Get Tournament Tough

There is no substitute for throwing yourself into the fire and finding your way out. There are things that happen in a tournament that do not happen during your matches at the club. By adding a referee, crowd, and different courts, lights, and match times, you completely change the dynamics of the game. There are plenty of players who are great at the club on Tuesday night, but cannot compete well in the situation of a tournament. It is truly a very different experience.

It is very difficult to simulate the pressure of tournament play. Because of this, the best way to practice under these conditions is to play tournaments. Enter and play everything you can handle if you are just starting out. Play two singles divisions whenever possible. Play the division in which you belong and the division above. If you are on the border of A and Open, win the A division and take your lumps in the Open. Do not fall into the trap of losing in the Open division and being mad enough about it to also lose your A match. The Open division is a whole other animal, so don't worry about it until you win the A's twice and get kicked up to Open only. You need the experiences you will gain in the divisions in which you are very competitive as a base to draw from when competing. I personally moved through the ranks too quickly, and skipped over the important lessons of being a seeded player, playing with a lead, and most importantly how to win. Don't make the same mistake.

For the advanced players, play the Open division and also play doubles. Playing doubles is good practice for singles because it teaches you to see the whole court. You must keep track of the other three players on the court and hit shots appropriate for the situation. There is no substitute for real life experience.

Be sure to chart your progress. Monitor why you win and why you lose matches. Try to learn not only from your losses but also from your wins. Most people have a tendency to gloss over the wins and look only at why they lost a match. Don't discount the knowledge and experience that wins provide, as well. Be conscious of what areas need work and what areas are solid. Pay attention to your fitness level and whether or not it is sufficient to get you through the finals. Most people do not have the benefit of a coach, so do the next best thing: Be your own coach. Give yourself the opportunity to improve by taking note of what needs to be worked on.

There is one way to simulate the pressure of a tournament--play for money. It doesn't need to be a lot of money either; some of my friends would nearly kill themselves trying to beat me and win a smoothie from the snack bar. However, there are two guys at my club who frequently play for $1,000 per game, but I wouldn't recommend that. Spot points if you're better, take points if you're not. Even things out and do battle.

Another key part of the equation is your fitness level. Consult a personal trainer in your area, or pick up a copy of my Fitness for Racquetball book at www.rbguru.com

One Month Out

Thirty days before a tournament, I would recommend you try to spend one day of each week doing the things you're already good at, just to stay sharp. Next, spend a day or two drilling if you can. If you could practice one day on your own and one day with a partner or a focused lesson with a Pro, this would be ideal. Now play a match with someone who is a full level below. This allows you freedom to work on things with a less pressure from your opposition. Be sure to play a match with someone who is better than you, also. This helps to pull your game forward. If you can't spend this many days working on your game, combine one of the practice sessions with the run-through of the things you consider your strengths. Work on things such as serve return and court position.

Keep in mind, you have four weeks before the tournament, so use your time wisely. Don't go to the club and sit waiting to play challenge court matches. Schedule a court and get your job done. Socialize after you're done, especially if court time is difficult to come by. Go to the club with a game plan and execute it. Show up early, warm up, stretch, and get ready to do what you need to do. Work on your weak areas; this is the only way to improve. This kind of discipline is necessary for success. Practice it, learn to think and live like a winner.

As far as your workouts are concerned, I would recommend that you train harder the second and third week of the month and taper off the last week before the tournament. You should play more than workout the week of the tournament anyway, so give your body a good chance to recover before the big event. You are not doing yourself any favors by coming into a tournament tired before the weekend starts.

The Week of the Big Event

It's the Monday before the tournament which starts on Friday night. Crunch time. Make sure you spend your time efficiently the next few days. Play a match with a lower level player on Monday night. Prepare for this match just like you are going to prepare for a tournament match this weekend. Simulate the tournament by showing up early, stretch, ride the bike, listen to music, whatever you would normally do at a tournament. Set aside a few moments to visualize the upcoming event. Whatever you are establishing as your pre-match routine, use it before your practice matches, too. You must practice your rituals and make them a consistent part of what you do. Be sure to jot down some notes on what you did well and what you need to work on over the next few days.

On Tuesday, work on the things you had written down from the night before. Practice with a partner if possible. This should be the hardest workout of the week, because you will want ample time to recover physically.

Wednesday night should be spent playing a match with someone equal to you or maybe a little better. Play a regular match (two games to 15 and a tie-breaker to 11, if necessary) and be finished for the night. I am not fond of playing six or seven games for practice, because most people tend to pace themselves and not worry about the fact that they just lost three out of the first four games. A good stretch afterwards is always an excellent idea. Find a fitness trainer, or someone else who is available, and get a really good stretch while you are very warm and loose after playing. Not only do you make the most gains in flexibility by stretching after you play, you also help to aid recovery and reduce stiffness in the muscles.

Thursday is optional. I usually like to have a very light workout on Thursday because I am used to playing or working out almost every day of the week. This is up to you. If you feel like resting, then rest. If you had a bad match on Wednesday, maybe playing a little on Thursday is a good way to rebuild some confidence in your shots. This is personal preference; if you are not sure, try something one tournament and try the opposite the next. See what is best for you as a competitor.

Listen to your body. If you are in need of rest, then rest. You will not do yourself any good coming into a tournament tired.

Something to consider: If you play at a club without glass wall courts or courts that are panel walls and you know the tournament will be held at a club where the courts are different than the ones you're used to, you may want to take a field trip and play on the courts where the tournament is being held. If you can't get to the actual tournament site, play on similar courts for your Wednesday match. This will help you adjust to the new surroundings of the tournament. A splat will bounce differently off a glass wall or a cement wall versus a panel wall, and serves certainly are affected by the make-up of the court. Be as prepared as possible; it's worth the price of a guest fee.

The main thing you want to do is be rested coming into the tournament. You are not doing yourself any favors by showing up tired, sore and dehydrated. If you start the tournament this way, it is unlikely you will catch up during the course of the event. Taking off one day to gain the rest and recovery you need is far better than grinding away blindly. Remember, you are not likely to get <u>that</u> much better the day before the tournament, anyway. Be sure you drink at least a gallon of distilled water on Thursday and again on Friday before you play.

One Hour before your Match

Usually there is very little time to warm up before your match. Courts are typically full during the course of a tournament, so I recommend warming up gradually for the hour before a match. I will arrive at the club about an hour before I play, go change into my playing clothes and start thinking about my match. I will grab a racquet, glove, and a ball (don't forget your eye-guards) and be ready to run on a court somewhere when the players are done after a match. Take advantage of the lag time and get on the court to hit a few smooth strokes, both forehand and backhand. If time permits, hit a few lob serves and some ceiling balls before the players for that court show up.

Once you get chased from the court, continue the sweat you're developing by running or riding a stationary bike. Maybe add in some foot speed exercises such as jump rope or line jumps. Now that you are warmed up from the inside out, grab your Ipod and find a place to stretch. Put on your warm-up jacket and spend a good amount of time stretching your legs and lower back. Listen to your choice of music. Choose your music appropriately--something upbeat if you need to wake up or something mellow if you're a little more amped than you think you should be. Visualize yourself playing the match--hitting the shots you want to hit and playing proper court position. Do your best to *feel* what you are picturing in your head.

Most of the time I like to be alone, from the time I am done running until I begin the match. I want no distractions before I play. Inform your spouse or family members that come to watch. They will understand. After all, they want you to win too. Don't let anything disrupt your preparation for your match.

Ten Minutes and In

When you are assigned to a court, try to get on the court as soon as possible. I like to be on the court without my opponent to hit some serves and cross court shots. Once your opponent arrives, start hitting down the line passes and straight in kills on your side of the court. When the time is right, switch and do the same on the other side. Start out by hitting shots at 50% speed and increase the speed until you are hitting shots at full speed. I like to warm up with an old ball; not one that is shiny and rock hard, but one that has been used before. The reason for this is that when the ref arrives and gives me the game ball, it seems that I am hitting the ball harder than before. This feels good to me, and it's a small confidence boost right before I start playing.

Now I am ready to go and hit the ground running, so to speak. A good start to a match is important. It is much better to be out in front than to be playing catch-up from the get go. Remember to be flexible in your preparation; the tournament director may want to speak to you and interrupt your warm-up, you may get bumped to another court, etc. Don't get superstitious or so dependent on the warm up process that you can't perform without a perfect warm up.

Exceptions to the aforementioned:

Sometimes I am a little more nervous before a match than others, and would prefer to talk to some friends and lighten the mood a little. I find this to be better sometimes than starting out too nervous and trying to settle down as I go. You can always tap into that energy if you need it because it is still there. You must learn to gauge what is best for you under each circumstance and act accordingly. The same routine will not be perfect for every situation you face.

How to Handle Pre-Match Nerves

There are several ways to deal with nerves before a match. Bear in mind that it is good to be nervous about the upcoming event. Wilt Chamberlin didn't feel ready for a playoff game until he puked his guts out in the locker room. The nervousness is a sign to your body to get ready for something. It will be highly alert and allow you to do things that you may not be able to do on a normal basis. But you must also understand that this excess energy can work against you if you do not use it properly. Over-swinging and slow feet are two sure signs of nerves and neither will help you win your match.

1. **Run your nerves away**. A good amount of physical exercise may be just the ticket to calm yourself down. Remember that you need to be in good shape if you plan on adding additional exercise *before* you play your match. Running, doing foot speed drills, jumping rope, or riding an exercise bike all may help to settle your nerves, but may also reduce your overall fitness.

2. **Controlling your breathing.** You must learn to breathe properly all the time, but especially under stress. You must breathe in through your nose and push your stomach **out** when you inhale. Most people do the opposite. Breathing properly will suck the air to the bottom of your lungs to the highest concentration of alveoli (the part that absorbs the oxygen from the air you breathe). This will assist the absorption of oxygen into your system, help you to slow your breathing and heart rate and to recover faster after a long rally. This is by far the most efficient way to breathe; it will keep you calm and centered, and facilitate clearer thinking. If you are hyperventilating, your thoughts are consumed by getting enough air into your body to

keep from passing out. If your breathing rate returns to normal quickly, you can move on to thinking about what you need to do next.

3. **Understand and accept the process.** Realize that pre-event nerves are your body's way of preparing for what is about to happen. Your system is gearing up for battle and is better prepared to handle the demand you are asking of it. Your brain secretes chemicals that enhance reaction speed, stamina and sometimes even athletic ability, so learn to use the feelings that well up inside you before a match. It does take practice but believe me, if these feelings disappear, you have a serious problem-- **burnout**. So embrace those butterflies and learn to use them to your advantage.

Mental Preparation for the Task Ahead

There are some things to consider in advance when playing a match:

1. Be sure to remind yourself why you are here. You are at this tournament to enjoy yourself, improve as a player, accomplish the goals you have set for this event, and learn from the experience.

2. If you are playing someone with whom you are good friends, or maybe even your doubles partner, work out some of the internal conflicts that you think may arise ahead of time. Do I want to beat this person? Will this affect our next match together? You both are there to win, so play fairly and do your best. Those thoughts seem silly now, but they do come up on occasion Deal with them in advance so they do not distract you during the match.

3. If you are playing someone you strongly dislike, rehearse some of the situations in advance so you will be better prepared to deal with them if and when the time comes. For example, if you play someone you expect to be in your way frequently, visualize yourself holding up and realizing that is better than forcing a shot from a crowded position. Understand that, overall, the calls do even out, so don't be afraid to replay a few rallies in lieu of tagging someone in the leg just because they didn't move in time.

There are times when you may need to establish that you are not going to let your opponent take advantage of your nice demeanor. I am not condoning blasting someone in the back after the first hinder in the match. I am suggesting that you speak up to the ref the first couple of times that it appears they didn't really try to get out of your way. The next step is to express your concern to your opponent. If the person is running into you before you finish your swing, it is dangerous for both of you. You are expressing concern for them as well as your right to an unimpeded swing. There are times, hopefully few and far between, where neither of the above suggestions will work. Ask for a new referee, someone who will call avoidable hinders. If that is not possible or is not helping, you are on you own as to what to do next. I'm not taking any responsibility for your actions, so don't bother mentioning my name while you're appealing your defaulted match with the tournament director.

If you are playing out of town and are playing a popular local player, expect the crowd to cheer for them and maybe even applaud your mistakes. Don't let it catch you off-guard when it seems like you are the only one who wants you to win this match.

1. If you play someone you know will slow the pace, rehearse your actions to accommodate this slower pace.
2. If you think these things through ahead of time, they will affect you far less during the match. Try to anticipate the common things that might occur and think in advance of the best way to deal with the situation(s).
3. If you play someone that stalls, argues, etc., try to rehearse these situations as well, so they do not catch you off-guard.

The Dreaded Referee

Why you should expect five bad calls per match:

Obviously, if you play tournaments, you also have to referee matches. You know what it's like; you've just lost a match, you're angry, tired, hungry, your feet hurt and you desperately need a shower. Not to mention, you have a doubles match to play in an hour. This is the last place you want to be. Well, bear in mind this is how your referee feels when he starts your match.

There will be times when the referee is totally blocked from the play, such as a *two bounce get* when your opponent dives forward. Sometimes the players have a much better perspective than the referee. You should not expect your opponent to over rule a call, ever. If they do, that is a bonus. Don't be surprised if they take the call. This is a tournament, not a club match and sometimes that affects people's judgment. Not everyone is completely honest.

If you make it through a match with only three missed calls, your ref did a great job. Tell them so. Racquetball matches are tough; we play a game that is one of the fastest sports on earth. Players are diving and sliding all over the place, and the situation does affect most refs' judgment. No one wants to call an avoidable hinder at 9-8 in the tie-breaker. If you plan on getting five bad calls per match and only get three or four, you came out ahead! If you get more than five, at least you were expecting some bad calls and were prepared to deal with them. For the most part, the calls do balance out in the end. The most important thing is that you prepare for the worst and don't let a bad call or two rattle you out of your positive mind-set.

How to Pick the Right Professional

The best players are not always the best teachers. Someone who is very athletically gifted may not identify with the average person's struggles with footwork or timing of the shots. Some players have a unique style that would be very difficult for most people to learn. I tried hitting forehands like Cliff Swain for a very short time. I actually had Cliff show me how he does it and tried it for about a week. My big toe ended up hurting because every time I hit the ball, I drove it straight down. His version of the forehand was not for me. In my opinion, he is too far over the grip and his swing leaves no room for error at all. His approach to the forehand takes world-class timing and it was apparent I do not have his abilities. It is too difficult to time the ball that perfectly every time.

The average club pro is someone who wants to teach lessons and/or run leagues in exchange for a free club membership. This may not be the person who is best suited to help you reach your goals. Ask around at tournaments or call the state director in your area to see if they have a good suggestion. Hopefully this book has answered most of your questions, but if not, here are some things to look for:

1. **Someone who knows what they are doing.** If you find some young hotshot who is swinging so hard he is coming out of his shoes and wants to teach you the same, that is a good warning sign. I recommend you look for someone who can do basic things well. If they seem to have a good grasp of the fundamentals, they may be just who you are looking for. Avoid someone with a "unique" style of play. There are some definite parameters to stay within in terms of mechanics.

2. **Someone who isn't just after your money.** If you find someone who seems to be dragging things out or who is just playing against you and charging you, this is a warning sign also. If you spend an entire hour on one thing and it was not your idea, this is probably a warning sign. I never like to teach that way because it is boring for the student and it takes time to get comfortable with a new technique. I don't feel the need to "do it till you get it right". You should be able to practice things on your own until you get them right.

3. **Someone who is unreliable.** If you find messages on your voicemail saying "Sorry I missed our lesson last night, I got busy with something else", find someone else.

4. **Someone who is not patient and encouraging.** The last thing you need is someone chastising you for "not listening to them".

5. **Consider attending a Racquetball Camp.** There are several quality Racquetball Camps offered around the country. Ask around to see which one will offer the right experience for you.

知识就是力量

Knowledge is Power

Off Court Training
for
Racquetball

Fitness for Racquetball

I must preface this section by saying that I am not a personal trainer, physical therapist, athletic trainer nor do I have any certifications in this field. I am sharing with you some of the basic things I did to raise my fitness level for tournament play. I would highly recommend that you consult your doctor and/or someone who is a qualified trainer before you do any of these exercises.

There are inherent risks involved in any training program. Be careful and use your judgment; if you have bad knees, weak ankles, a bad back or any other area that gives you problems, tailor your workouts accordingly.

Racquetball is an anaerobic sport. This means that the activity is not a sustained activity like running a 10K, but a burst and recovery type of endeavor. This is why I am sharing these exercises; hopping on a stationary bike and riding at a steady pace for an hour will improve your overall fitness, but it not improving your fitness for racquetball.

To uncover my full workout program and tap into one of my biggest assets as an athlete, check out my book "Forge your Body". You can find it at www.rbguru.com

Stationary Bike

The appropriate way for a racquetball player to use the stationary bike is to do sprints. Sprints are difficult, so you will have to work your way into it. Do a five minute warm up at a low setting to get started. Then find an appropriate level to start with and use the manual setting at level 5 and sprint for 20 seconds. Now reduce the level and cruise for 40 seconds. Try to do this for 15 minutes, but let me warn you it is tough. The goal of this exercise is to build up to the point where you can do this exercise at a higher level (10 or 12) and also switch the sprint time to 40 seconds and the recovery time to 20 seconds. If you can build up to do sprints for 40 seconds and recover almost fully in the remaining 20 seconds, for a duration of 20 minutes, you will be well prepared for a racquetball match.

Sit in the seat and grind!

Do not stand up.

Jumping Rope

This is a great exercise for many reasons; one reason is that jumping rope will help increase your footspeed. Another reason is that this exercise is difficult, and causes your heart rate to elevate quickly and your legs to tire. Your lower legs are what overcomes all of your body's momentum, so you must train accordingly. Racquetball is a very demanding sport on the lungs and the lower body, so this exercise is a great way to increase the stamina in both areas.

Train so you can do 500 single jumps at a time. This should take you about 5 minutes if you don't miss. There is a certain Professional Tennis Player who used to measure her fitness level by gauging her jump rope stamina. She could do 600 single jumps in 3 minutes. I have yet to match that mark—505 was my closest number so far, but I am still working on it. ☺

A great variation on this exercise is to learn to do doubles as well. One of my favorite exercises is to do 25 doubles and then 20 push-ups. Work your way up to doing 3 sets of this exercise to target your shoulders, chest and legs all at once.

Plyometric Hops

This is another good exercise for the development of speed and stamina in the lower legs. I have chosen a four inch high foam device that allows me some room for error if I miss a step. The foam will give if I land on it and I shouldn't get injured as easily. I used to do this with a step aerobic stair, but you cannot miss with that. If you do, you are likely to roll an ankle or worse.

Anyway, do these facing the side and also jumping front to back. I recommend two sets each direction for 15 reps, and build your way up from there. "Bounce" off of your toes as quickly as possible for maximum speed and effect of this exercise.

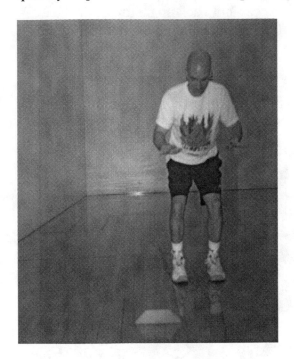

Box Jumps

If you play at a health club with a fitness center, it is likely they may have a set of plyometric boxes or at least a weight bench you can use for this next exercise. This is a great exercise to develop balance and strength/stamina in your legs.

Choose a box height which you can jump onto the top of comfortably without crashing. Be sure the box is not going to slide each time you land on it. I push the box against the wall so it won't move, but this means I must control my landing each time to avoid smashing my pretty face into the wall. I like my nose where it is, thanks. As the picture illustrate, start in a squatted position similar to returning serve. Now jump and land on top of the box, and jump back to the starting position again. Strive to bounce right back up on top of the box without resting on the floor. Start with two sets of 10 reps, and build up the number of reps before graduating to a taller box.

Lunges

I know, I know, these are not a lot of fun! But they are a very good exercise for a racquetball player to do. The lunge, when done properly will perfectly simulate the position your legs should be in when you hit a forehand and a backhand. This is an excellent way to train your legs for match and tournament play where you are doing these moves over an over for up to five days in a row. Do these exercises after you play or on an off day. Do not do these before you practice or play; your legs will be wobbly and you'll end up practicing poor form.

I like to do these on the court. Start with your hands behind your head or your arms extended for better balance. Begin the exercise against the back wall, step out with your right leg, striding just far enough to end up with your legs in a 90 degree position. Do not put your heel down at any time during this exercise. Now raise up and with good balance stride out with the left leg and repeat this exercise to the front wall. Turn around and lunge back to the back wall; do not waiver, rest or cheat during this exercise, it is well worth the pain.

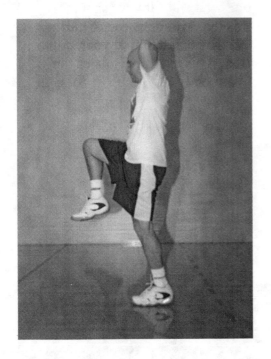

Core Body Exercises

Racquetball involves a large amount of twisting and rotating your mid and upper body. You should increase your body's capacity to do these motions more quickly and with more strength. The following exercises are a good beginning to adding to your overall core strength.

The Crunch

A basic crunch is performed by starting lying on a mat on your back. Raise your knees so your feet are flat on the floor. Place your hands behind your head and lift your shoulder blades off the mat. Strive to keep your nose pointed towards the ceiling instead of curling up. These should be treated as two different exercises. Feel the contraction of your stomach, hold for a second or two, then return to your starting position. This exercise isolates the stomach muscles and adding to the stamina of this area of your body. Work up to doing at least 100 of these at a time.

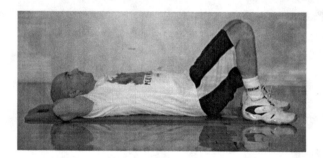

Rotary Torso

If you are fortunate, your club has one of these machines, and you can do this exercise at length in a locked in position. Use the one that has you rotating your upper body and not your legs. This simulates your swing much more effectively.

If you do not have one of those machines, or you prefer this method, do Russian Twists from a seated position on the mat. Touch the ball down on each side of you, as far back behind you as you can reach. Rotate quickly side to side, and do it til it burns, then do ten more. Strive to do three sets of 40 touches.

Leg Lifts

Lie flat on your back, and place your hands under your butt. Your legs should be extended, knees locked. Lift your feet off the ground about 8 – 10 inches, hold and then gradually lower your heels back to two inches off the ground. Do not touch them down, that is resting, save that for later. Do sets of 10 -15 reps, and work your way up from there.

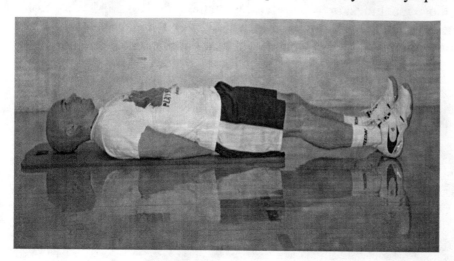

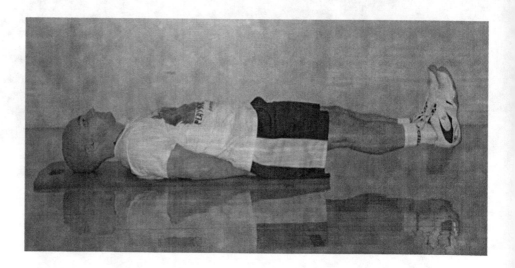

Supermans

To make sure we do a little something for the lower back, roll over on the mat and lay on your stomach. Your arms should be extended out in front of you, and your legs extended. Now arch your back so that you raise as much of your torso and your legs off of the mat as possible. Hold this position for five seconds, then return to your starting position. Count this as one rep, and strive to do two sets of 15 reps.

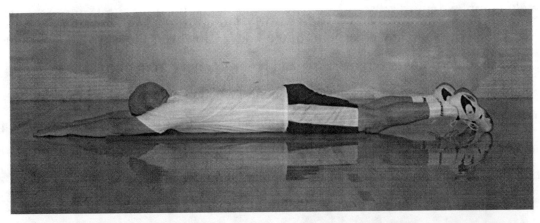

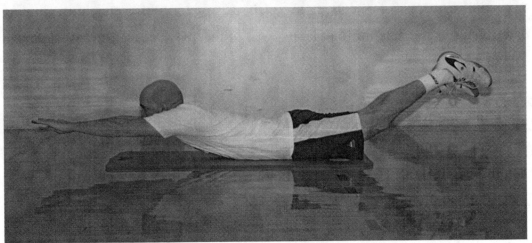

Injury prevention and rehabilitation of the shoulder for racquetball players.   By Mitch Bruning, P.T.

As the old saying goes, "an ounce of prevention is worth a pound of cure" was never more accurate when describing the shoulder joint. The glenohumeral (shoulder) joint is an extremely complex unit of muscles, tendons, cartilage, and bone. It allows for more mobility and diverse activity than any other joint in the body. However, these advantages come at a price. The shoulder joint is very unstable and prone to injury from overuse in activities such as racquetball. The shoulder has very little bone to bone contact, and relies heavily on the muscles and tendons that comprise it. To complicate matters, the oxygenated blood supply is less than adequate when compared to other joints in the body. It is of critical improatance to maintain the strength and function of the scapular, shoulder blade, and rotator cuff muscles. In sports that incorporate a significant amount of repetitive movements of the shoulder, the athlete becomes suspect for conditions such as rotator cuff tendonitis, impingement syndrome (bursitis) and anterior joint laxity. All of the above cause pain, weakness, and los of function.

What does this mean to a racquetball player? If you spend a minimal amount of time on injury prevention, you can dramatically reduce the probability of falling victim to any of these conditions. Taking 15 to 20 minutes three to four times a week will put you on the right track to hopefully preventing a shoulder problem.

As previously mentioned, the shoulder joint gets poor blood supply. It is necessary to spend five to ten minutes in an anaerobic activity like jogging or biking to increase circulation and consequently oxygenate the shoulder muscles. These are very small muscles that are going to be conditioned and need higher repetitions as opposed to more weight. The focus will be on two separate components: 1. the scapular muscles and 2. the rotator cuff muscles. The scapular muscles are the ones in the upper portion of the back that surround your shoulder blade. The rotator cuff is deeper in the shoulder complex and function to hold the arm in the socket and provide for rotation of the joint. All of the muscles work together to stabilize the shoulder and allow the hand to perform "fine" movements, such as accurately hitting a ball with a racquet. Please do the following exercises with light weight and strive to add reps before adding weight.

Scapular Strengthening Exercises—Latissimus Dorsi Pulls

Be sure to pull to the bar in front of your head only!

Seated Row

Be sure to keep your spine straight when doing this exercise.

Resisted shoulder adduction

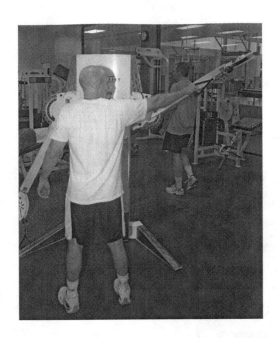 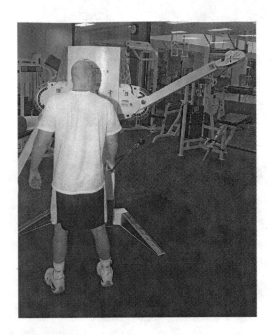

Be sure not to lean into this exercise; keep good form and posture throughout this exercise.

Again, use lighter weights and strive for higher reps with this exercise.

Resisted external rotation in adduction – 90 degrees

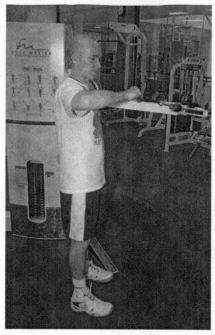

A strong rotator cuff is essential for the demands of racquetball. An injury will rarely heal on its own, so prepare correctly and help avoid this common injury.

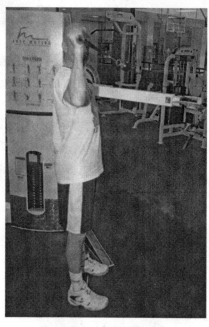

Rotator Cuff

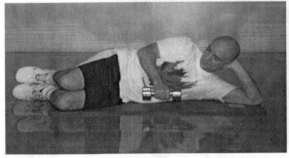

Do each of these exercises with a light dumbbell and high reps.

A commonly asked question is "what can I do if I experience a shoulder injury during a tournament?" Numbness and tingling radiating down the arm and/or constant aching through the night are indicators that you may have a significant injury and should not continue. However, if you determine that your symptoms will not prohibit you from continuing, here are a few tips that can help you:

1. Take an extra 10 to 15 minutes to warm up and get more blood flowing into that area.
2. Use a topical analgesic such as Flexall 454 or Icy Hot to promote superficial circulation.
3. After completing your match, I would suggest icing your shoulder for 20 minutes on and 20 minutes off for a total of 90 to 120 minutes.
4. Take a recommended dose of an anti-inflammatory medication.

If you have an injury, discretion is the better form of valor. I highly recommend that you consult your physician and/or physical therapist for a comprehensive evaluation and treatment. This should be done before you attempt any of the protocol in this book.

Thank you and good luck!

Mitch Bruning, P.T.

If you are interested in additional strength training and weight lifting for racquetball, consult a qualified personal trainer. You want a program geared for burst and recovery style training, not necessarily one that packs the pounds on your frame and ups your max bench, dude. Again, use some common sense in addition to the guidelines in the book.

Reading Material-- the following books are a must read:

Winning Ugly	Brad Gilbert
Optimum Sports Nutrition	Dr. Michael Colgan
In Pursuit of Excellence	Terry Orlick, MD
Mental Toughness for Tennis	Dr. James Loehr
Inner Game of Tennis	W. Tim Gallwey
The Book of Five Rings (you can skip the intro.)	Miyamoto Musashi
Journey to Ixtlan	Carlos Castaneda
It's not about the Bike	Lance Armstrong
The War Of Art	Steven Pressfield

I have read many books on the subject of sports psychology and performance, and I got a lot out of the few books listed above. The books that seem a little esoteric for the sport of racquetball, probably are. However, like I have said throughout this book, this is about competition and the life-altering journey that the pursuit of a dream can be. You will need to be armed with as much information about <u>yourself</u> as you can get your hands on, and that is why I included the others on the list.

Role Models for Competition

Brad Gilbert – Professional Tennis. Former coach of Andre Agassi, lifetime Grand Slam Tennis Champion

Brad Gilbert is a self-admitted meager talent. He knows his strokes aren't pretty, he is never mentioned when discussing the quickest players on Pro Tennis Tour, and his name is quickly forgotten when it comes to "flashy players" that sold lots of tickets. Yet in spite of this, he beat everyone on Tour during his time, with the exception of Ivan Lendl. I guess Lendl had his number. In contrast to a quote made by John McEnroe stating Gilbert to be "a caveman who found a tennis racquet," he made over $4 million dollars and reached a world ranking of #4 at one point in his career.

What Gilbert did possess, more so than anyone on tennis tour, was a phenomenal ability to summon the talents he did have at the appropriate time. He was a master of transferring pressure to the opposition, playing the percentages and capitalizing on errors made under pressure by his opponents. He was one of the best at squeezing the life out of the other player. Brad Gilbert also was a true work horse; he was blue collar through and through. He worked hard to achieve what he did. Yes, I realize that everyone at that level works hard, but he worked harder. He had to--he did not possess the talent that a lot of other players did.

Another thing to add to your game that Mr. Gilbert can teach us is the ability to prepare. He had a very specific pre-match routine, and kept a book on everyone he had ever played. He

had a set of rules he always abided by, such as never serving first in a match, and he was prepared for everything from a headache to a broken shoelace. Nothing was left to chance.

Lesson: If you work hard toward your goals, prepare and stick to your game plan, you can accomplish great things.

Jimmy Connors – Professional Tennis

Jimmy was amazing, he was the player I always wanted to be. Jimmy was very talented; he had the best return of serve in the game until Agassi came along. He had the ability to whip every crowd into an absolute frenzy. Jimmy Connors was like a conductor directing the entire orchestra. He was the bad guy when he played against Borg and the good guy when he played McEnroe. At 38 years old, he made the semi-finals of the US Open. He was unbelievable during some of the matches in his later years because he used to feed off the crowd to win. Everyone in the stadium would be frantically cheering for him by the end of the match. If you have ever seen the matches from the US Open when Jimmy played Patrick McEnroe and Paul Haarhuis, you know what I am talking about. Each match was over four hours of mass hysteria, and Jimmy was conducting the crowd like he was a band leader.

As an opponent, you never knew what Jimmy would bring into a match, whether it would be screaming at the umpire or sharing a joke with the entire section on his side of the stadium. He had to stay focused under the craziest conditions imaginable and that is very difficult for most players.

Jimmy was also known for never accepting a loss very well. He always said "I never lost a match, I just ran out of time before I solved the problem." The bigger the situation, the more pressure there was, the more Jimmy loved it. This carried him all the way to the top.

Even today he ranks as one of the top five players with the most weeks spent at number One.

> *Lesson: Learn to love the pressure of a big match; develop the guts and desire to take the last shot and make things happen versus letting your opponent's mistake give you the match. Take charge of the situation.*

Lance Armstrong – 7 time Tour De France winner

Two and a half years before the 1999 Tour De France, cyclist Lance Armstrong was diagnosed with testicular cancer. This was not a small hitch in his training schedule, this was his life at stake. Lance chose the more difficult of the two treatments, knowing if he survived that he would recover faster and have a better chance of leading a normal life. He did survive, and began to do what was thought to be impossible. He began to train. He had to change his way of riding and training due to his muscle loss during his hospital stay. He turned the "problem" into an advantage and went to France to compete in one of the toughest tests in sport. Not only did he win the Tour De France but he dominated, winning numerous stages of the race and building up to a 7:00 minute lead over every other racer in the field. He followed it up by winning the 2000 Tour De France also.

Lesson: Never, ever give up. No matter what the circumstances, you can prevail if you chose.

I love the NIKE commercial with Lance when he talks about it being *his* body. " I can do what I want with it, push it, study it, tweak it, listen to it. People want to know what I'm on. What am I on? I'm on my bike six hours a day bustin' my ass, what are *you* on?

Tiger Woods –PGA Touring Professional

This seems like an obvious choice when it comes to role models, but many people fail to realize just how hard Tiger works. This is a guy who practices in the rain, high wind, and other miserable conditions just so he knows what to expect when he is playing a PGA event. Tiger Wood's father and mother both helped him prepare for the journey he is on. The ability to focus so intently that nothing distracts him, flash a brilliant smile in between shots, and speak so eloquently about his peers that he continually out plays is a master at work. I am glad to be witness to the history he is making; rapidly working his way towards Jack Nicklaus' Major Title record.

Lesson: Anything and everything that Tiger does pushes him closer towards perfection. Never lose the desire to practice, hone your skills, and showcase your abilities on the biggest stages.

Jim Courier – Professional Tennis

Jim Courier has been a stalwart of Davis Cup Tennis. He has answered the call when other players have shaken their heads no. He rose to the number one ranking for over a year between the 1991-93 seasons, but some of his best tennis was played in service of the USA's Davis Cup Team. Even recently, when his ranking has dropped out of the top 50 in the world, he has summoned some incredible tennis to beat tough players. In the past few years, I have watched Jim come from behind to beat Marat Safin of Russia (2000 US Open Champion) after being down 2-0 and 5-1 in their match. The challenger showed signs of nerves trying to serve out the match and Courier jumped all over him. He broke serve, held serve, and broke again to pull out the third. He hung around long enough to get into a position to win the match. By the fifth, he had turned the tide so much that he ended up winning the fifth set easily. In 1999 Davis Cup play against the British team, Courier beat two top ten ranked players, Tim Henman and Greg Rusedski, in consecutive matches. Courier played double tough when it counted, beating Henman 9-7 in the fifth and Rusedski 8-6 in the fifth. He did a nearly perfect job of waiting for good opportunities and capitalizing on them when they appeared. He did not make bad choices, go for too much, or make any service errors during the crucial stages of those matches. Awesome!

Lesson: If you can play well under pressure, you can hang with anyone.
Develop the capacity to be a clutch player.

When playing a better player, put the burden of proof on them. Make them prove to you that they are the better player, not the other way around. Play within your capabilities and don't give anything away. This will increase your chances of performing well.

Commentary on the Maniacal Pursuit of a Dream

Don't fall into the trap of becoming so consumed with your pursuits that you are miserable every time you lose a match or have a bad practice session. I was somewhat guilty of this when I played on Tour. I would train very hard, I feel "harder" than almost anyone, and show up at a tournament only to get my ass kicked by someone who was a better player than I. I would get very depressed. Since I don't drink, I used to eat a lot of chocolate desserts on Friday nights at the tournaments. I usually felt better by the time I got home, but sometimes it would linger for a week or more.

Bear in mind, this game is not a reflection of your worth as a person, your social standing, or anything else you may perceive to be at risk when you lose a match. It is ultimately just a game. You must be happy with who you are, regardless of what happens on the court.

Conclusion

The basic premise of this book is this: Hard work and a solid game plan will take you a long, long way. I am not as physically gifted as some of the people playing racquetball at the highest level, and I am one of the smallest guy to ever play full time on the International Racquetball Tour. I reached the Professional level with the information presented in this book and a good work ethic. I knew what I wanted to accomplish and I worked and worked until I achieved my goals.

This book was written to help others reach their personal goals in racquetball, regardless of what those goals may be. I am a big believer in the idea of success in one area of life can breed success in other areas. It is by no means a guarantee, however. Some of the most talented athletes I know are absolute "hack" human beings. I wish you the best of luck in your endeavors.

Darrin Schenck

PS…feel free to email me at Darrin@rbguru.com. I'd love to hear from you.

Appendix A

About the Author

I am from a small town in Pennsylvania. I moved to Phoenix when I was 12 years old. My father was a great wrestler in high school and beyond. I thought it was my destiny; to be a good wrestler, get a college scholarship, and "make something of myself." As a freshman in high school, I broke a bone in my neck trying to earn a spot on the wrestling team. This forever altered what I thought was my future. What does a guy with my physical attributes do to follow an athletic dream?

I was 15 years old the first time I ever saw a racquetball court. My Uncle Brad took me to play racquetball and announced he would spot me 15 points to 21 and still win. Well, he was right. Not once, but twice. Well, this was not acceptable to me, so I began to practice. I walked across the street from my house and played at the park next to Paradise Valley High School. I am proud to say that one month later, he only spotted me 10 points and only beat me two out of three. Well, I was hooked, and thus the story begins.

I weighed 134 pounds when I played on Tour. I do not come from an affluent family, far from it at times. I began playing racquetball at age 15, which is 7 years later than the average Touring pro playing during my time on Tour. But not everything was stacked against me. I am quick; have good eye-hand coordination, and a strong work ethic. I probably worked harder than almost anyone in the game for most of my career. I <u>made</u> myself into a Pro Tour Player. I found a way to turn everything in my favor, and make everything push me towards my goals. I spent three years in the Top 25 in the world, with a career high season end ranking of #18 in the world.

I have experienced some of the ultimate highs and ultimate lows the sport has to offer. The first racquetball tournament I ever played in was the 1986 Pro-Am at the Arizona Athletic Club. I was the only player to lose twice in the novice division. That's right--twice. I got crushed in my first match 15-2, 15-1. Later in the same day, I was sitting on the bleachers pouting when the tournament director found me. She said there was a no-show and asked if I wanted to play again. I got beat just as badly the next time, too. Between my two beatings that day, I watched the Pro's play and was absolutely amazed. All the guys were great players, some of them had gorgeous women with them, and I thought they made a lot of money playing a game for a living. This was a day that changed my life. I decided to join them.

A mere 11 years later, one of my best friends had an out-of-body experience and gave me the most embarrassing loss in the history of professional racquetball. I lost to Louis Vogel in my home town 11-0, 11-0, 11-0, with my doubles partner refereeing the match. Louis would have beaten a lot of players very badly that day. I just happened to be the lucky recipient. But the important thing is, I survived the experience and learned from it. (There was a nice little article in Racquetball magazine about this incident.)

On the other side of the coin, I have had some fantastic wins in my career. One of my favorite stories is when I beat Steve Lerner (of Riverside, CA) in Las Vegas. I had followed Steve's career for most of the time I had played racquetball. The guy I took a few lessons from as a beginner once told me I would be a Steve Lerner-type player some day. In one of the best matches I have ever put together mentally and emotionally, I beat Steve 14-15, 15-3, 11-10. Every rally was the same the entire match--Lob Z the forehand, ceiling ball, ceiling ball, ditto, ditto until one of us would shoot a backhand and try to end the rally. At 10-10 in the tie-breaker, I ended up rolling a backhand kill right down the middle of the court from

39.5 feet. It was awesome. Unfortunately, no one was cheering for me. When I hit that shot, I was jumping up and down celebrating and everyone who was watching just kind of shrugged their shoulders and walked away. Oh well, I don't play for anyone but me anyway.

In my four years on the International Racquetball Tour, I also kept my amateur status and played local tournaments. I played about 28 events a year during that time, from 1995 to 1999. In that time frame, I was 134-12 in tournaments in Arizona, winning several tournaments each year in my hometown. There were weekends that I would fly to a Pro-Am and play Thursday afternoon and Thursday evening if I won the round of 32 match. If I lost, sometimes I would jump on a plane and come home to play a tournament in Phoenix. One of my best "double dips" was Labor Day weekend in 1998. I played the Stockton Pro-Am, and got a forfeit in my round of 32 match on Friday. At 8:30 PM I played Cliff Swain, the Number One player in the world and lost in four games. I played the best match I have ever played against Cliff, losing a close first and winning the second. This was the first match in which Cliff had lost a game before the semi's all season. Unfortunately I did lose, and then had to ref the next match between James Mulcock and Sudsy Monchik, which also went four games. Dinner at midnight, then back to the hotel. At 9:00 AM Saturday morning I bummed a ride, from a very gracious Greg Freeze, to the airport to fly home and play in the Super 7 Series tournament in town. The first flight was canceled, so I called Ben Simons, the tournament director to tell him I couldn't make it back in time for my noon match. He was kind enough to delay my starting time and I caught the next flight out. My girlfriend picked me up at the airport, we hit a drive-thru at a Chinese restaurant, and I ate in the car on the way to the club. I walked into the club and on the court, beating a good player three straight. I ended up winning the tournament, beating a "fresh out of retirement" Jimmy Floyd in the finals. Thank goodness he was rusty; I was awfully tired by then!

In my professional career I was able to win games against some of the best players the game has ever seen. I beat Marty Hogan in an exhibition match, took games off of Cliff Swain, Sudsy Monchik, Andy Roberts, and many other names that you may recognize. Not bad for a guy who is small in stature, started the game late in life, and had very little formal coaching along the way.

In addition to playing on the IRT, I also was the photographer for Killshot magazine, wrote Pro Tour Update articles for the magazine, was the IRT official stringer for two seasons, and was the emcee and contest organizer for the first three US Open Racquetball Championships. Now do you recognize me?

I reside in Phoenix, AZ where I teach and assist other players in reaching their goals. I have been teaching and coaching players for the past 15 years. I am the coach for the ASU Racquetball Team; in my first year my Girl's team won a National Championship and I led the Team to a 2nd Place finish overall in 2007. We were able to follow this up in 2008 with a Girl's Runner Up finish, and a #6 finish for the Team. I would list these as one of my most satisfying racquetball accomplishments. I was voted as 2008 Coach of the Year at the awards banquet at the Intercollegiate Championships, and am proud of my team for reflecting hard work and dedication which I have tried to instill. I also coach a lot of individuals who play tournaments, and really enjoy watching them in action. I am in the Commercial Interiors business for my day job. In my spare time I enjoy fly fishing and the outdoors, and play a little golf, but it's tough with a name like mine :-)

知识就是力量
Knowledge is Power

Appendix B

Things I Did to Help My Career:

--Worked with a financial planner to form an L.L.C. (limited liability company) as a sponsorship vehicle. This helped to relieve *some* of the pressure of winning matches to pay rent.

--Worked with a very knowledgeable trainer to ensure I was as physically prepared as possible.

--Studied martial arts to improve fitness, flexibility, self control and self discipline.

--Worked with a hypno-therapist to improve performance in competition.

--Found a practice partner who could help me reach my goals.

--Did a trade out with a massage therapist to aid in recovery from training and competition.

--Worked with Andy Roberts on how to play at the professional level.

--Arranged a schedule so I could train and play every day.

--Graduated from the Sports Vision Therapy Program at the Advanced Vision and Achievement Center, Scottsdale, AZ.

—**Surrounded myself with successful, hardworking athletes and people who are encouraging and supportive. I have found you tend to act like the people around you, so choose your friends and associates accordingly.**

Some of My Favorite Quotes...

I like to post signs and notes all over my home, car, and office to constantly remind myself of my goals. If I need help to retrain a certain thought process or whatever, I find having quotes or passages in front of my face is a good way to keep these thoughts constantly on my mind. The following are some of my personal favorites. Feel free to use any that suit you.

"A person should not be measured by what they accomplish, but what they overcome."

> Johnny Miller--the last PGA golfer to win 8 tournaments in one season before Tiger Woods did it in 1999.

"Don't try harder, try easier."

> George Brett--Lifetime .300 hitter and MLB hall of Fame player

"Pain is temporary, Victory is forever"

> anonymous

"I never lost a match, I simply ran out of time before I solved the problem"

> Jimmy Connors

"Minimalism is the key to greatness"

> Darrin Schenck

"I am the Lizard King, I can do anything"

> Jim Morrison

Pretty much anything Vince Lombardi said

The Book of Five Rings   by Miyamoto Musashi

Today is victory over yourself of yesterday; tomorrow is victory over lesser men.

Immature strategy is the cause of grief. Do not let the enemy see your spirit.

The primary thing when you take your sword in your hand is your intention is to cut your enemy, whatever the means. To cut and to slash are two different things. When you cut your spirit is resolved.

Teach your body strategy.

In order to beat more skillful men, train according to the Way, not allowing your heart to be swayed along a sidetrack.

In single combat, if an enemy is less skillful than yourself, if their rhythm is disorganized or if they have fallen into evasive or retreating attitudes, we must crush them straight-away, with no concern for their presence and without allowing them space for breath. It is essential to crush him all at once. The primary thing is to not let them recover their position even a little.

The Way of strategy is straight and True. You must chase the enemy around and make them obey your spirit.

Deliberately, and with a patient spirit, absorb the virtue of all this and from time to time raising your hand in combat."

Tao of Jeet Kune Do   by Bruce Lee

"The consciousness of self is the greatest hindrance to the proper execution of all

physical action".

An Art is a means for acquiring Liberty.

It is not daily increase, but daily decrease---Hack away the unessential

To know oneself is to study oneself in action with another.

To become a Champion requires a conditioning of readiness that causes the individual

to approach with pleasure even the most tedious practice sessions.

A golden rule is to never use a more complex movement than necessary to achieve a desired

result."

Miscellaneous

You must be able to determine your ability relative to your opponent's ability. This is
difficult because that relationship is always changing; day to day and minute to minute.

You must decide what tactic or method to use in order to carry out your game plan, and then
assess the success of the plan throughout the course of a match.

Act the way you want to become and you will become the way you act.

Whether you think that you can or you cannot--you're right.

Concentration is doing what your doing while your doing it.

Worry is a thin stream trickling through the mind. If encouraged, it will become a channel into which all thoughts are drained.

Quitting is a permanent solution to a temporary problem.

If someone speaks badly of you, live so no one would believe it.

When strict with oneself, one rarely fails.

Excellence does not remain alone, it is sure to attract neighbors.

Watch what you say, and whatever you say--practice it.

When an archer shoots for nothing, he has all his skill. If he shoots for a prize of gold, he sees two targets--he is out of his mind. The skill has not changed but the prize divides him. He cares. He thinks more of winning than of shooting; and the need to win drains him of power.

You can eat an elephant a bite at a time.   Eco-challenge racer

The size of your heart is far more important than the size of your body.

People, by and large, become what they think about themselves.

"Winners and losers are self-determined but only the winners are willing to admit it."

> John Wooden--Nine time national collegiate
> basketball championship coach

Fine athletes in every sport know the importance of trusting their mechanical skills. And they do it regardless of the result they achieved on their last attempt.

"Every hunter has ultimately to learn the way himself...the truest hunter must go beyond rote lessons to a degree of knowledge that has become thoroughly ingrained, become an instinctual quality of his being, something beyond mere consciousness. He must, finally, be able to cross over from *understanding* to *knowing*. That is what ultimately cannot be taught."

> **Thomas McIntyre**
> **The Way of the Hunter.**

Further Acknowledgments

The following is a list of people to whom I wanted to take the time to say thank you from the bottom of my heart for your support. Here, in no particular order, is the list:

Scott Winters, Mike Wong, Tom Cain, Louis Vogel, Andy Roberts, Doug Ganim, Hank Marcus, Dr. James R. McDonald, Bob Key, Michael Schenck, Nancy Schenck and George Bolan, Greg McBride, Dr. Richard Glonek, Tim McClellan, Richard Shields, Paul Scott, Dr. Richard Nichols, Bruce Cole, Dr. David Foley, Dr. Arnold Calica, Steve Bernard, Chuck Theisen, Steve Oliverio, Lou Spelts, Greg and Elizabeth Thybulle, Richard Mackey, Chuck Kennedy, GrandMaster Andrew Bauman, Dr. Janice and Vic Shayne, Ben Simons, Donna Angelopolus, Darin DeCesare, Ron Grimes, Amy Wishingrad, Harvey Klein, Mark Mulzet, Brian Schilling, Mike Jensen, Don Powell, Jon Cohen, Steve McBride, Tim Borgwordt, Jeff Bell, Warren Anderson, Mitch Bruning, Jim "JR" Rosania, Russell Curtis, Larry Desorbo, Connie Wong, Michael and Gini Hartzmark, Don Thomas, J. Brand, Gary Clark and HoneyBear's Bar-B-Que, The Village Racquet & Health Club.

Printed in the United States
111968LV00002B/397-454/P

9 780615 189598